RESOURCE
EXTRACTION
AND
PROTEST
IN PERU

PITT LATIN AMERICAN SERIES

John Charles Chasteen and Catherine M. Conaghan, Editors

RESOURCE EXTRACTION

AND

PROTEST IN PERU

MOISÉS ARCE

UNIVERSITY OF PITTSBURGH PRESS

To my wife, Jen, and to my daughters, Isabel, Marcela, and Emilia

Published by the University of Pittsburgh Press, Pittsburgh, Pa., 15260
Copyright © 2014, University of Pittsburgh Press

10 9 8 7 6 5 4 3 2 1

Library of Congress Cataloging-in-Publication Data
Arce, Moisés.
Resource Extraction and Protest in Peru / Moisés Arce.
    pages cm — (Pitt Latin American Studies)
Includes bibliographical references and index.
ISBN 978-0-8229-6309-7
1. Natural resources—Political aspects—Peru—History. 2. Protest movements—
Peru—History. 3. Peru—Economic conditions—1968- 4. Peru—Politics and
government—1980- 5. Democracy—Peru—History. 6. Political parties—Peru—
History. 7. Peru—Social conditions. I. Title.
HC227.5.A73 2014
333.80985—dc23
                              2014023326

CONTENTS

ACKNOWLEDGMENTS

This book project began in the mid-2000s when I was an assistant professor at Louisiana State University. I wrote a paper examining the protests against the privatization of electricity in the city of Arequipa in southern Peru, which happens to be my hometown. At that time, the mobilization appeared to be an isolated event, and there was not a lot of literature discussing protest movements against the deepening of economic liberalization policies. As such protests spread over Peru, as well as several other countries in Latin America, I began to study them more closely. It has been an exciting opportunity, and I have learned a great deal. This book summarizes this intellectual journey.

As I reflect on the themes addressed in this book, I cannot help but think about the hundreds or thousands of people who have been affected by these mobilizations. I wish that the Peruvian political system would offer them a better way to channel their demands and resolve their disputes. Yet despite these limitations, I know that their actions have made a difference, and the country's political life is better off because of their resilience in the streets.

I am extremely thankful for the guidance I received from my advisors at the University of New Mexico, Karen Remmer and Kenneth Roberts. As I have said repeatedly to friends and colleagues, I was very fortunate to learn from them, and words are insufficient to express how much I owe them for what they taught me over the years. I also thank my colleagues at the University of Missouri for their continuing support. Particularly, Margit Tavits and Robin Best helped me to clarify and formulate better arguments about the relationship between political protest and parties.

A number of students were also helpful in seeing this book to completion. Paul Bellinger brought a lot of energy to the early stages of this project. It was great working with him, and our trip to Peru was a lot of fun. Marc Polizzi provided valuable research assistance. I first met Marc when he was a sophomore, and now several years later he is getting ready for comps. Marc has been very close to this book throughout that period, and I am thankful for all of the work he has done in improving the manuscript. Caitlin McCormack and Jane Silcock did an excellent job in researching the case study materials of this book. I also thank Daniel Encinas, Carolina Garay, Yamilé Guibert, and Félix Puémape, all of whom I have kept busy in collecting the data shown in this book. I greatly appreciate their efforts.

For their knowledgeable recommendations over the years, I express sincere thanks to Paul Almeida, Carew Boulding, Melissa Buice, Marisa von Bülow, Maxwell Cameron, Julio Carrión, Catherine Conaghan, Gustavo Flores-Macías, Candelaria Garay, Mariel García, Samuel Handlin, Wendy Hunter, Javier Iguiñiz, María Inclán, Wonik Kim, Steven Levitsky, Jorge Mangonnet, Cynthia McClintock, Carlos Meléndez, Alfred Montero, Maria Victoria Murillo, Gabriel Ondetti, Indira Palacios, Aldo Panfichi, Maritza Paredes, Aníbal Pérez-Liñán, Pablo Quintanilla, Roberta Rice, Catalina Romero, Federico Rossi, Eduardo Silva, William Smith, Alberto Vergara, Takeshi Wada, and Kurt Weyland. I have also benefited from numerous anonymous reviewers from various journals, and I acknowledge their suggestions here and elsewhere. Naturally, responsibility for any remaining shortcomings in this book rests solely with me.

I would like to thank the following organizations for providing the funding that made my research possible: the Louisiana State University Council on Research Summer Stipend Program, the Louisiana State University College of Arts and Sciences, the University of Missouri Research Board, and the University of Missouri Research Council. In Lima, the Facultad de Ciencias Sociales of the Pontificia Universidad Católica del Perú (PUCP) and the Instituto de Estudios Peruanos (IEP) provided valuable support. I especially thank Eduardo Dargent and Martín Tanaka for their assistance in getting the data collection for this project off the ground.

I also would like to extend my sincerest thanks to Joshua Shanholtzer, Carol Sickman-Garner, Alex Wolfe, and the editors at the University of Pittsburgh Press. They were extremely supportive in moving this project along, and it has been a pleasure to work with them.

To my late parents, Jaime Arce and Haydeé Esquivel, I appreciate the times we spent together. Our discussions about Peruvian politics still make me laugh. To my family in Arequipa, Cajamarca, and Lima, I thank you all for making my visits fun and busy. My deepest gratitude goes to my wife and daughters for keeping me cheerful on this journey.

INTRODUCTION

At the dawn of the twenty-first century, the face of Latin American democracy looked remarkably different than it did in the late 1970s. This new face revealed the political ascendancy of indigenous people, the growing political representation of women, and the rise of several leftist presidents across the region. These developments were not disconnected; rather, they were aided—some more than others—by an unexpected source of popular contention: political protest.

Following Latin America's third democratic wave, which began in 1978, much of the scholarly literature anticipated that conflicts involving political society would be resolved through representative institutions that evoke compliance among the relevant political forces. However, starting in the late 1980s, several Latin American countries began to experience a generalized rise in protests directed toward a broad range of policies collectively known as "neoliberalism" or "economic liberalization." These antimarket mobilizations were effective in rolling back unpopular economic policies, such as the privatization of government utilities, pension systems, and social services, as well as projects that sought to expand the extraction of natural resources. Waves of street protests also forced embattled popularly elected presidents to leave office early. With greater autonomy from parties and state institutions, protest movements joined together numerous groups from civil society, including indigenous peoples, women's organizations, students, human rights groups, landless small farmers, and informal and unemployed workers, as well as traditional labor unions. They displayed a broad repertoire of contentious activity, such as attacks on governmental buildings and politicians' houses, national and provincial roadblocks, banging pots and pans, setting up camps in civic squares, and urban riots. Most of these mobilizations were short-lived, with specific political objectives or policy demands. The resurgence of protest changed the face of Latin American politics, igniting a "second historical process of mass political incorporation" (Roberts 2008, 38) that breaks from the traditional pattern of state-led, vertical incorporation of labor unions, which characterized the first inclusion period (R. B. Collier and Collier 1991).[1]

One way to organize the different episodes of contention surrounding economic liberalization policies is by recognizing the presence of one general cycle of mobilizations with surging and receding waves of protest. In this cycle, the first wave corresponds to the protests against the austerity measures of the 1980s. These austerity policies primarily sought to restore macroeconomic discipline and produced the so-called IMF riots that Walton and Seddon (1994) and others have studied. The second wave follows the deepening of economic liberalization policies starting in the late 1990s, as seen in the protests against the privatization of utility services (e.g., water in Bolivia in 2000, electricity in Peru in 2002), and the mobilizations against the expansion of the extractive economy (e.g., gold in Peru in 2004, gold in Guatemala in 2010) as a consequence of growing volumes of foreign and domestic investments in the natural resource sector.

Prior research on the rise of antimarket contention in Latin America has emphasized the grievances or economic threats that are associated with the implementation of economic liberalization policies (Almeida 2009; Silva 2009). These grievances or threats emboldened popular sectors and middle classes to mobilize and represent the common origin behind different episodes of antimarket mass mobilization (Silva 2009). Indeed, grievances can be a powerful mobilizing force, as seen recently in Argentina, Bolivia, Ecuador, and Venezuela, when aggrieved social groups forced presidents who supported neoliberal policies to resign. These mobilizations also contributed to the election of political forces interested in reforming neoliberalism.

This book departs from existing studies on the resurgence of antimarket protest in Latin America in two important ways. First, moving away from broad conceptions of economic liberalization that take into account several areas of policy reform, the book disaggregates the grievances or threats that are associated with economic liberalization by looking at one particular set of mobilizations that are tied to a specific type of economic policy: the extraction of natural resources. Resource extraction is the "face of neoliberalism" (Slack 2009, 117) in many Latin American countries and has accelerated as a consequence of privatization policies and the loosening of restrictions on foreign direct investment.

The study of protests over natural resource extraction is theoretically important because existing research has argued that natural resources, such as oil and minerals, represent "structurally significant" (Selby 2005) resources that make up a key aspect of a developing country's political economy. These resources are a central source of revenue for a country's economic development and state building, in particular, and an important component in industrial capitalist economies, in general. In addition, research has shown that natural resource extraction especially affects the rural poor and produces grievances among the local population due to insufficiently compensated land expropriation, environmental degradation, and inadequate job opportunities. Insofar as the extraction of "structurally significant" natural resources is pivotal to a country's political economy, protest over these policies has the potential to shape the long-term development strategy of the state.

Second, existing research on the revival of antimarket protest in Latin America has also taught us much about the factors that shape mobilizations cross-nationally. However, generalizations drawn from aggregate national data that conceal significant heterogeneity and complexity within countries are problematic, particularly when variation in patterns of mobilization across subnational boundaries is abundant (Boulding 2010; Murillo and Ronconi 2004). This forces us to ask: What political factors account for the subnational unevenness of popular contention? Why do apparently similar resource-abundant subnational units within the same national democratic regime have different levels of protest? And under what conditions are protest movements, which initially appear to be localized, segmented outbursts, more likely to produce substantive gains for aggrieved groups?

In this book I probe these questions for the case of Peru, which represents an interesting puzzle for the theoretical literature on the rise of antimarket contention in Latin America. On one hand, existing research portrays Peru as a prime example of political "quietism" in the wake of economic liberalization (Silva 2009; Rice 2012). The reasons posited for the country's demobilizing response to neoliberalism are many and range from the effects of the insurgency war, which made it difficult to build organizational and coalitional capacity, to the absence of political associational space, particularly during the Fujimori decade (1990–2000), and finally to the severing of class-based organizing during the shift toward economic liberalization policies.[2] On the other hand, more recent research acknowledges the country's rising wave of social protest (Arellano-Yanguas 2008; Cameron 2011a), such as the student demonstrations in resistance to Fujimori's authoritarian encroachments during the late 1990s, the protest against the privatization of water in Arequipa in 2002, and the mobilization in opposition to the opening of the Amazon for development in Bagua in 2009. However, this same literature argues that these mobilizations remained scattered and disarticulated and were of little national importance. These mobilizations did not result in a process known as "scale-shift" (McAdam, Tarrow, and Tilly 2001), in which isolated instances of protests transform into growing streams of mobilization, including the types of national-level protest movements that have emerged in neighboring and ethnically similar Andean countries like Ecuador and Bolivia.

Contrasting these perspectives, Peru has had more than its share of mobilizations at the subnational level and currently has the third-highest percentage of respondents reporting protest participation in the Latin American region (LAPOP 2008). The Peruvian case reveals both demobilization (mostly during the 1990s) and mobilization trends over time. Moreover, subnational units, which are very similar to each other when it comes to the abundance of natural resources and other attributes like geographic location and population, have experienced different levels of protest. For these reasons, the Peruvian case represents an ideal laboratory to explore the factors that influence the variation of popular contention across space and time. It can be helpful to evaluate the relative weight of economic explanations (following Silva's understanding of the grievances or threats associated with economic liberalization) vis-à-vis political explanations (following the main arguments of this book). More important, if subnational mobilizations over the extraction of "structurally significant" (Selby 2005) resources are shaping the trajectory of the state, that process has important ramifications for understanding the political consequences of popular contention elsewhere in the Latin American region.

As shown in later chapters, the extraction of natural resources in Peru has led to an impressive economic expansion, aided by record-high commodity prices and the growing Chinese demand for raw materials. Peru is among the world's top-five producers of minerals like gold, silver, copper, lead, tin, and zinc (Gurmendi 2008). The country also stands out as having the highest concentration of the world's top mining companies in the region (Oxfam America 2009). Mining has been the main driver of recent economic growth and is a key source of government revenue—government officials increasingly see mining as "the agenda of national development."[3]

To be clear, other Latin American countries, such as Argentina, Bolivia, Venezuela, and Ecuador, have also experienced sizeable export bonanzas. As several studies have documented (Mazzuca 2013; Weyland 2009), the bonanzas have helped to strengthen the power of leftist governments. In these four countries, state actors have not only weakened democratic institutional checks and balances but also asserted their control over the revenues from natural resources in varying degrees. And by making the state the main beneficiary of the boom, state actors have engaged in several redistributive political projects. All together, the economic "good times" have led to what Sebastián Mazzuca (2013) has termed "rentier populism." However, there are several factors that set Peru's export growth apart from the experiences of these neighboring countries. First, rather than leading to a concentration of power in the executive, the export boom has overlapped with a process of decentralization (McNulty 2011). The election of subnational governments (hereafter regional governments) that began in 2002 created centrifugal forces for the distribution of mineral rents (chapter 3) and thus placed constraints on executive powers. Second, in the post-Fujimori period the private sector has been (and remains) the main driver of the expansion of the extractive frontier. And rather than succumbing to the "urge of expropriation" (Mazzuca 2013, 111), state actors have sought to protect the country's "investment grade" by maintaining an open-door policy toward foreign direct investment and thus secure greater volumes of capital in the natural resource sector. In all, the financial reputation of the country served to immunize actors against the temptation for expropriation of natural resources.

Democracy and Political Competition under Weak Institutions

Drawing on an original protest event dataset of mobilizations and extensive fieldwork, my findings suggest that natural resource-based grievances or threats do not monotonically generate greater levels of protest, as a grievance-centered approach would suggest. Rather the broader political context in which protests emerge provides a better explanation for the incidence of popular contention. The salience of political conditions as central to explaining antimarket mobilizations follows contributions from the literature on social movements, in particular political process theory (Tarrow 1998; Tilly and Tarrow 2006). Political process theory presents three frameworks—political opportunity, resource mobilization, and framing processes—to examine the dynamics of protest movements, as well as the impact of these movements on their environment. These three frameworks are now largely seen as one approach rather than three separate analytical lines. The political conditions that occupy this book include the moderating role of democracy, the quality of institutional representation as embodied in political parties, and finally the level of political party competition. Collectively, these political conditions capture the formal dimensions of political opportunities (the first framework from political process theory), which are useful to explain the national and subnational variation of protest movements across geography and time. In contrast, resource mobilization and framing processes (the other two frameworks from political process theory) are central to explaining the larger effects of protest movements on their environment. In this manner, this book pushes political process theory toward increased interactivity, showing that in the presence of favorable political conditions, as in the context of democracy (political opportunities), societal actors can build a master frame linking resource extraction and injustices (framing processes), which, in turn, allows for the building of broad coalitions with diverse sets of actors (resource mobilization).

Scholars of social movements have long argued that in the absence of a political environment that affects the incentives for people to undertake collective action (Tarrow 1998), people with intense grievances may pose only negligible challenges to existing regimes. In this book, I emphasize the systemwide political opportunities advanced by democratization that are favorable for popular mobilization.[4] Compared to autocracies, democracies foster collective mobilization by relaxing repression (Francisco 2009), encouraging associational life, and opening channels of popular participation (Almeida and Johnston 2006). Conceptualizing democracy as an opportunity for mobilization helps explain the variation of protest across countries and over time, showing that the political opportunity for protest is generally higher in democracies compared to autocracies (Tilly and Tarrow 2006, 66). This political opportunity approach can also help us understand protest trends in Peru over a period of time. For instance, the decade of the 1990s under Alberto Fujimori was comparatively less democratic, with fewer outlets for political representation, compared to other periods, and had fewer mobilizations as a result. This approach, however, is only part of the larger puzzle on the resurgence of antimarket mass mobilization. Looking at the level of democracy cannot easily explain the subnational variation in patterns of mobilization that exists within countries, including Peru, particularly when this level remains time invariant.

To refine our understanding of the link between democracy and protest at the subnational level, I emphasize another formal dimension of political opportunities, as well as a central attribute of democracy, that can help us untangle how and why democracy affects mass mobilizations—political competition. Electoral theories of democracy have long posited that political competition is the primary source of government responsiveness (e.g., Key 1966; Fiorina 1981). Through electoral rewards and punishments, political competition offers citizens the opportunity to influence the behavior of politicians, and by altering the behavior of politicians, political competition enhances the connection between public preferences and government output. Because of this, political competition advances the best hope for government responsiveness. All other things being equal, political competition induces greater responsiveness among politicians; therefore, when the level of underlying political competition is higher or more pronounced, politicians should be more likely to enact policies that are designed to reduce protest activity, thus increasing their popularity at election time.[5]

However, there are several reasons why political competition may fail to enhance government responsiveness and hence reduce protest activity. Chief among them is poorly developed political parties and party systems. As I explain in chapter 1, weakly developed parties and party systems are likely to impair the mechanisms of responsiveness and accountability that are typically associated with political competition and thus strain the connection between public preferences and government output. This observation is consistent with research that has shown that weak institutions create incentives to use protest as an instrument to influence those who govern (Arce 2010b; Machado, Scartascini, and Tommasi 2009).[6] The implication here is that the mechanisms of responsiveness and accountability that are tied to political competition vary according to the context where competition takes place. Therefore, rather than assuming that the connection between competition and responsiveness always functions smoothly in any given case, the effects of competition on protest should be more carefully scrutinized. The Peruvian case provides an ideal setting to examine the effects of political competition on protest in the presence of weak institutions, given that the country's party system has been plagued by political outsiders since 1990 (chapter 2). Relatedly, the Peruvian case has broad implications for several new democracies characterized by fluid and fragmented electoral politics.

By bringing political conditions back into the analysis of antimarket contention, this book seeks to fill a gap in the existing theoretical literature on the social consequences of economic liberalization. The book's understanding of democracy as an opportunity for mobilization suggests that democracy following Latin America's third democratic wave is becoming gradually more meaningful, allowing collective actors to use channels outside the traditional ballot box to contest or modify the economic reform policies that affect their lives. This book's emphasis on the effects of political competition sums up a central attribute of a multidimensional concept, such as democracy. It allows us to examine the salience of political conditions at the subnational level and further see how the institutional context where competition takes place affects the connection between public preferences and government output. On balance, the book's new take on protest—subnational political competition—sheds light on a broader theme—democracy—and builds on earlier work that has shown that greater levels of political competition are associated with lower levels of subnational protest in Argentina (Arce and Mangonnet 2013) and Bolivia (Arce and Rice 2009).

Returning to political process theory, whereas the formal dimensions of political opportunities—democracy and party competition—allow us to explain the variation of protest events across time and space, the focus on resource mobilization and framing processes is key to explaining the broader impact of protest movements on their environment. In fact, in several mobilizations against the extraction of natural resources, agriculture-based organizations as well as nongovernmental organizations (NGOs) were instrumental for the emergence of successful collective action and, as such, reflect the salience of organization and mobilization resources. This book also shows how strategic framing allowed opposition groups to build associational power and collective power. The former refers to the ability of subordinate social groups to create new organizations or recast existing ones (i.e., organizational capacity), and the latter implies the ability of subordinate social groups to forge coalition building across new or recast organizations (i.e., coalitional capacity).[7] To summarize, insofar as political conditions were favorable, both framing processes and resource mobilization transformed localized, segmented outbursts against resource extraction into larger opposition movements that affected national-level politics.

A Subnational Comparative Analysis

Democracy, economic reforms, and even waves of antimarket contention are territorially uneven processes. For this reason, this book exploits the methodological advantages offered by a subnational comparative analysis (Snyder 2001). As is widely known, large-N cross-national analyses facilitate statistical testing of theoretical arguments, but usually at some cost in terms of the quality of measures used. Case studies, in contrast, provide detailed, rich treatments of causal mechanisms, but at some cost to the ability to cope with rival theoretical arguments and generalization. A subnational comparative analysis reduces these familiar methodological compromises by allowing both statistical control and detailed knowledge. A subnational comparative research design allows us to hold constant cultural, historical, ecological, and socioeconomic conditions, while allowing subnational variation in the variables of theoretical interest.[8]

More important, a subnational comparative analysis provides greater sensitivity to within-nation heterogeneity and complexity, which is largely concealed in aggregate national data. The tendency to unreflectively gravitate toward national-level aggregate data and national units of analysis—a tendency that Stein Rokkan (1970) calls "whole-nation bias"—has contributed to a misinterpretation of cases, which can potentially distort causal inferences and skew efforts at theory building (Snyder 2001, 94). In Silva's (2009) analysis, for instance, Peru emerges as a divergent case that did not experience large episodes of popular mobilization, yet the country has seen more than its fair share of social protests at the subnational level, and some of these protests have had important effects on national politics and policies (Arce 2008).

The mobilizations against the extraction of natural resources, which again are typical of the second wave of protest against economic liberalization, also allow for a theoretically oriented and controlled comparison of protest movements, as these movements have similar objectives and forms of mobilization. Up until now, case studies of protests against resource extraction have generated a wealth of descriptive detail, yet the main task of this book is to advance a generalized understanding of the factors that determine the dynamics of protest movements against resource extraction.

This book goes beyond most recent work on the consequences of economic liberalization under democracy on three fronts. First, the bulk of existing literature to date focuses almost exclusively on broad conceptions of economic liberalization that encompass several areas of policy reform. Yet there is ample reason to believe that the factors shaping the different types of antimarket mobilization are indeed quite distinct. This book improves existing research by examining the societal consequences of a specific market policy: natural resource extraction. Second, existing research has primarily drawn conclusions based on outcomes aggregated at the national not subnational level. This book's subnational comparative research design pays attention to within-nation heterogeneity and complexity to formulate better causal inferences on the factors that shape protest activity locally and over time. It provides the detailed region-by-region (akin to states in other countries) information on protest that would allow us to test many of the leading perspectives on contentious politics. Third, and finally, rather than emphasizing grievances or economic threats as the main determinant of the emergence of antimarket mobilization (e.g., Silva 2009), this book focuses on the broader environment where protest takes place (democracy), as well as a central attribute of democratic regimes that leads to greater government responsiveness (political competition). The effects of political competition on antimarket protest vary according to the institutional setting where competition takes place. Overall, the empirical evidence reveals that a political environment favorable for mobilization allowed social subjects in Peru to influence and reshape extractive policies that were initially executed in a top-down, centralized fashion. These findings emphasize the importance of looking beyond the initial alignment of interests surrounding extractive activities to explore their political consequences as they unfold over time.

A subnational comparative analysis of Peru, which is new among the Latin American scholarship, allows us to study the consequences of what James C. Scott (1986) characterized some time ago as "everyday forms of [collective] resistance" on the trajectory of the state. As one would expect, countries like Argentina, Bolivia, Ecuador, and Venezuela have received considerable scholarly attention by students of contentious politics because in these four countries mobilizations led to the removal of presidents who supported neoliberal policies. However, the removal of chief executives as an indicator that mobilizations were consequential is a high threshold to cross and runs the risk of chilling the debate on the societal consequences of economic liberalization. As such, the presence and consequences of mobilizations in other countries like Peru, which approximate the normal pattern across the Latin American region, could be quickly dismissed or ignored altogether. This, of course, is not ideal because as Silva (2009) reminds us, protestors are social subjects with substantive demands, not undifferentiated mobs who solely promote public disorder. And as the Latin American experience suggests, political leaders who choose to ignore protestors' demands do so at their peril (Silva 2009, 283).

As noted earlier, the austerity protests of the 1980s, as well as the protests against the deepening of economic liberalization during the late 1990s, could be seen as two protest waves within a generalized cycle of contention. While addressing the factors that help explain this general cycle of mobilization (chapters 1 and 2), the latter wave occupies the bulk of this book. In particular, the analysis centers on the mobilizations against the expansion of the extractive frontier because of their structural importance to a developing country's political economy.

In the first half of the book, I pay attention to the variation in forms of protest across and within countries to shed light on the factors that help explain the resurgence of contentious activity in Latin America, in general (chapter 1), and Peru, in particular (chapters 2 and 3). Chapter 1 presents the central argument of this book and the theoretical framework that informs it. Building on political process theory (Tarrow 1998; Tilly and Tarrow 2006), in particular the political opportunities literature, it emphasizes the political conditions that influence societal responses to economic liberalization: democracy and political competition. Chapters 2 and 3 examine the temporal and spatial variation of protest within Peru. These chapters draw on an original protest event dataset recording thirty-one years of mobilizations based on the Peruvian print media (Arce 2014). Chapter 2 explains the varying political environments that have produced distinct waves and modes of popular contention beginning with the country's transition to democracy in 1980 until 2010. The analysis presented in this chapter indicts two commonly asserted explanations of protest trends in Peru. Those arguments involve the state of the economy and the presence of political violence. The data reveal two broad waves of protest since Peru's transition to democracy: one during the early to mid-1980s and the other one in the mid- to late 2000s. In congruence with the emphasis on political conditions from chapter 1, only the level of political liberalization was comparatively similar across these two cycles of protest.

Chapter 3 examines the relationship among resource wealth, political conditions, and protest across Peru's twenty-five regions. This subnational comparative research design corrects for the national bias of the existing literature. It allows us to coalesce changing patterns of mobilization and demobilization within a single country and control for ecological, cultural, and socioeconomic conditions to a far greater extent than is usually possible in studies that compare national units, all of which helps us to formulate better causal inferences of the factors that shape protest activity locally and over time. This chapter finds that the relationship between protest and subnational political conditions is closer than that between protest and natural resource rents, which can be seen as a useful indicator of resource-based grievances.

In the second part of this book, and following the contributions of the scholarship on resource mobilization and framing processes, I analyze the effects of mobilizations on the trajectory of the state. In particular, I pay attention to the conditions under which protest movements—that initially appear to be territorially segmented mobilizations—are more likely to produce substantive gains for aggrieved groups.[9] The focus is again on resource extraction because of its "structural" importance to the broader sustainability of economic liberalization policies, in general, and the Peruvian economy, in particular. Chapters 4, 5, and 6 analyze and compare three episodes of large-scale popular contention with widely varying impacts on national politics: Tambogrande, Mount Quilish, and Bagua. The three chapters trace the origins of these mobilizations from their initiation to the current period. Mobilizations against resource extraction like Tambogrande, Mount Quilish, and Bagua are also the most common type of social protest in Peru today (Arce 2008; Defensoría del Pueblo 2012) and "are among the most serious problems that confront" the country, given the importance of resources for the national economy.[10]

The mobilization in Tambogrande (chapter 4) in the Piura Region of northern Peru was the first to invoke a popular referendum in opposition to mining. This strategy, which was neither legally sanctioned nor authorized by the national government, has been replicated in other protests and with the same political objective. Tambogrande thus influenced the repertoire of contention nationally. Similarly, the mobilization in Bagua (chapter 6) in the Peruvian Amazon region forced the national government to recognize Convention 169 of the International Labor Organization (ILO), which advances consultation and participation rights on behalf of indigenous peoples on issues that affect them. Peru ratified this agreement as early as 1994, but it had never been enforced. In August 2011, the government of Ollanta Humala approved the "Law of Prior Consultation," aligning national laws with ILO Convention 169 and requiring national and foreign companies to seek prior consultation on development projects in indigenous lands.

The mobilization in Mount Quilish (chapter 5) in the Cajamarca Region stopped the expansion of the Yanacocha mine, the second-largest gold mine in the world. The Yanacocha mine has been subject to sporadic protests due to environmental contamination, including a mercury spill, poor rapport with local communities over land and water rights, and the distribution of rents generated from mining. Violent protests against the expansion of the Yanacocha mine continue to this day, and Mount Quilish is emblematic of the hundreds of mobilizations against resource extraction in Peru. In several of these protests, leaders of NGOs opposed to mining have been elected to political office and may draw on their organizational and institutional resources to steer mining projects in different directions than previously planned. The comparative analysis presented in chapters 4, 5, and 6 shows that waves of subnational natural resource contention strengthened democracy in Peru by pushing for social inclusion, popular consultation mechanisms, and other forms of grassroots participation. They also influenced the trajectory of the state by channeling a greater distribution of rents from the extraction of natural resources toward subnational units and sensitizing exploration and mining companies on practices involving corporate social responsibility.

The conclusion reexamines the distinctive societal impact of economic liberalization and the democratizing consequences of popular contention. It assesses the usefulness of a controlled comparison at the subnational level and how it helps to formulate better inferences regarding the factors that shape subnational contention across space and time. It extends the insights developed in this book to a wider range of cases in Peru and in other countries. It concludes by revisiting the impact of resource extraction on national politics.

ACRONYMS

ACPI   Agencia Peruana de Cooperación Internacional (Peruvian International Cooperation Agency)

AF   Alianza para el Futuro (Alliance for the Future)

AIDESEP   Asociación Interétnica de Desarrollo de la Selva Peruana (Interethnic Development Association of the Peruvian Rainforest)

ANGR   Asamblea Nacional de Gobiernos Regionales (National Assembly of Regional Governments)

AP   Acción Popular (Popular Action)

APRA   Alianza Popular Revolucionaria Americana (American Popular Revolutionary Alliance)

APRODEH   Asociación Pro Derechos Humanos (Association for Human Rights)

BRGM   Bureau de Recherches Géologiques et Minières (Bureau of Geological and Mining Research)

CAAAP   Centro Amazónico de Anthropología y Aplicación Práctica (Amazon Center of Anthropology and Practical Application)

CAN   Confederación Nacional Agraria (National Agrarian Confederation)

CAO   Compliance Advisor Ombudsman

CCP   Confederación Campesina del Perú (Peasant Confederation of Peru)

CEPES	Centro Peruano de Estudios Sociales (Peruvian Center for Social Studies)
CGTP	Confederación General de Trabajadores del Perú (General Confederation of Peruvian Workers)
CNDDHH	Coordinadora Nacional de Derechos Humanos (National Coordinator for Human Rights)
COICA	Coordinadora de las Organizaciones Indígenas de la Cuenca Amazónica (Coordinator of Indigenous Organizations of the Amazon Basin)
CONACAMI	Confederación Nacional de Comunidades del Perú Afectadas por la Minería (National Confederation of Peruvian Communities Affected by Mining)
CONAIE	Confederación de Nacionalidades Indígenas del Ecuador (Confederation of Indigenous Nationalities of Ecuador)
CONAP	Confederación de Nacionalidades Amazónicas del Perú (Confederation of Amazonian Nationalities of Peru)
CONFIEP	Confederación Nacional de Instituciones Empresariales Privadas (National Confederation of Private Business Institutions)
CPC	Corporación Cerro de Pasco (Cerro de Pasco Corporation)
CRF	Comando Rodrigo Franco (Rodrigo Franco Command)
CTAR	Consejo Transitorio de Administración Regional (Transitional Regional Board)
DAR	Derecho, Ambiente y Recursos Naturales (Law, Environment, and Natural Resources)
DL	*decretos legislativos* (legislative decrees)
EIA	*estudio de impacto ambiental* (environmental impact report)
ENP	effective number of parties
FDVST	Frente de Defensa del Valle de San Lorenzo y Tambogrande (San Lorenzo Valley and Tambogrande Defense Front)
FDVT	Frente de Defensa del Valle del Tambo (Tambo Valley Defense Front)

FEDEPAZ	Fundación Ecuménica para el Desarrollo y la Paz (Ecumenical Foundation for Development and Peace)
FNTMMSP	Federación Nacional de Trabajadores Mineros, Metalúrgicos y Siderúrgicos del Perú (National Federation of Miners, Metal and Steel Workers of Peru)
FPV	Frente para la Victoria (Victory Front)
FTA	free trade agreement (*tratado de libre comercio*)
GRUFIDES	Grupo de Formación e Intervención para el Desarrollo Sostenible (Training and Intervention Group for Sustainable Development)
IBC	Instituto del Bien Común (Common Good Institute)
ICMM	International Council on Mining and Metals
ILO	International Labor Organization
IMF	International Monetary Fund
INEI	Instituto Nacional de Estadística e Informática (National Institute of Statistics and Informatics)
IU	Izquierda Unida (United Left)
MCLCP	Mesa de Concertación de Lucha Contra la Pobreza (Roundtable for Poverty Reduction)
MEM	Ministerio de Energía y Minas (Ministry of Energy and Mines)
MERCOSUR	Mercado Común del Sur (Southern Common Market)
MIDIS	Ministerio de Desarrollo e Inclusión Social (Ministry of Development and Social Inclusion)
MMC	Manhattan Minerals Corporation
MRTA	Movimiento Revolucionario Túpac Amaru (Tupac Amaru Revolutionary Movement)
OAS	Organization of American States
ONPE	Oficina Nacional de Procesos Electorales (National Office of Electoral Processes)
PMSP	Programa Minero de Solidaridad con el Pueblo (Mining Program of Solidarity with the People)
PNP	Partido Nacionalista del Perú (Nationalist Party of Peru)
PPC	Partido Popular Cristiano (Popular Christian Party)
SCC	Southern Copper Corporation

SER	Asociación de Servicios Educativos Rurales (Association for Rural Educational Services)
SERVINDI	Servicio en Comunicación Intercultural (Intercultural Communication Services)
SNMPE	Sociedad Nacional de Minería, Petróleo y Energía (National Society of Mining, Petroleum, and Energy)
SPDA	Sociedad Peruana de Derecho Ambiental (Peruvian Environmental Law Society)
SUTEP	Sindicato Único de Trabajadores de la Educación Peruana (Sole Union of Workers of Peruvian Education)
TC	Tribunal Constitucional (Constitutional Tribunal)
UNOPS	Oficina de las Naciones Unidas de Servicios para Proyectos (United Nations Office for Project Services)
UPP	Unión por el Perú (Union for Peru)

PART I
THE FRAMEWORK

CHAPTER 1

RETHINKING THE CONSEQUENCES
OF ECONOMIC LIBERALIZATION

What are the societal consequences of economic liberalization under democracy? One perspective that has become front-page material in recent years evokes an image of a "backlash" against economic liberalization and globalization. Protestors from various sectors of civil society in several Latin American countries have ignited a cycle of popular resistance against the economic threats associated with economic liberalization policies (Almeida 2009; Silva 2009). Reminiscent of the "IMF riots" (Walton and Seddon 1994) that gripped the region during the 1980s, mass civic revolts have rolled back unpopular economic liberalization policies, even forced embattled promarket presidents to leave office early (Hochstetler 2006). Economic liberalization thus appears to have revitalized protest activity.[1]

This popularized "backlash" picture, however, is at odds with the conventional wisdom that associates exposure to worldwide competition with material insecurities and other demobilizing changes for popular subjects (Kurtz 2004; Silver 2003; Oxhorn 2006). As nations aggressively compete with each other to attract footloose capital, market forces are thought to homogenize policies and other economic institutions. This convergence has propelled a "race to the bottom" in labor standards, which in turn has severely weakened and fragmented popular subjects. Concomitantly, exposure to worldwide competition has allegedly resulted in a "powerless" postglobalization state with constrained capacities particularly in the areas of monetary and fiscal policies (Ohmae 1995; Strange 1996), and as such, the existing literature has argued that the state no longer represents a worthy target of popular mobilization. Thus the impersonal forces of economic liberalization produce political apathy and ultimately discourage protest activity.

Given the contradictions between widely publicized protest events and existing theory, this chapter reexamines the social consequences of economic liberalization under democracy. In the first half of this chapter, I review the contending theoretical perspectives on the relationship among economic liberalization, democracy, and protest: depoliticization and repoliticization. Building on political process theory (e.g., Tarrow 1998; Tilly and Tarrow 2006), this chapter shows how the repoliticization perspective helps us understand the national and subnational dynamics of protest movements across geography and time, as well as the impact of these movements on their environments. The repoliticization perspective, as discussed below, draws attention to the salience of political conditions in an area of research that has traditionally dwelled upon the influence of economic factors or conditions. In the second half of this chapter, I apply political process theory to the sets of research questions that motivate this book, which include the political conditions that help explain (a) the national variation of protests across countries, (b) the subnational variation of protest within democracies, and finally (c) the impact of protest movements on their environment.

Protest and Democracy during Latin America's Market Era

The relationship among economic policies, political democracy, and protest activity has been the subject of inquiry by several well-known Latin American scholars (e.g., D. Collier 1979; O'Donnell 1973). O'Donnell (1973) argued that economic crises resulting from the exhaustion of import substitution industrialization policies, and the economic reforms pursued to resolve them, ushered in an explosion of popular mobilization and class conflict that made bureaucratic authoritarianism an attractive option for powerful segments of society. According to this classic literature, then, the primary threat to democracy was the hypermobilization of collective actors in response to economic reform. Other work pointed out that democracies, with their emphasis on elections and political rights, enhanced the disruptive capacity of social forces (Crozier, Huntington and Watanuki

1975). In many ways, the revival of protest in the region mirrors the popular conflicts of this classic literature, insofar as economic policy, be it import substitution industrialization or economic liberalization, has been politically contested. However, the preoccupation with stability and order that characterized those studies has been relaxed. As Cleary (2006, 41) puts it, "protest politics, including strikes, demonstrations, and roadblocks . . . are seen as a legitimate form of civil disobedience within a democratic system, rather than a direct challenge to the system itself." In keeping with Cleary's observation, the 2009 Latinobarómetro survey reported that on average 92 percent of Latin American respondents viewed street mobilizations as a normal part of a democracy, a 29-percentage-point increase from the 63-percent response recorded in 2008 (Latinobarómetro 2009).[2]

The recent literature on the societal consequences of economic liberalization advances two competing views on the linkage among economic reforms, democracy, and protest. Depoliticization scholars emphasize the disorganizing effects of economic liberalization on popular subjects and do not expect democracy to revitalize collective action. Recently, however, this conventional wisdom has been challenged on a number of grounds by several studies documenting the revival of protest activity, in the Latin American region as well as other countries in the world. These repoliticization studies seek to explain how in some cases collective actors adapt to economic liberalization and how in other cases new actors and new forms of collective activity have emerged in opposition to these economic changes.[3] The implication from the repoliticization view is that collective action in the aftermath of economic liberalization simply changes, rather than vanishes altogether, as the depoliticization view would have it.

The Depoliticization Perspective

The literature arguing that the primary effect of economic liberalization is depoliticization expects a "generalized pattern of decline in mobilization" (Kurtz 2004, 289) as economic liberalization moves forward. This literature emphasizes the consequences of chronic economic crises and their often far-reaching and swift promarket resolutions, such as increased poverty and inequality, higher levels of unemployment, and lower standards of living (e.g., Agüero and Stark 1998; Oxhorn and Ducantenzeiler 1998; Oxhorn 2009; Kurtz 2004; Holzner

2007). These economic conditions are said to hurt the collective capacity of popular subjects and produce, among other things, anomie, disorder, and societal disorganization (e.g., Zermeño 1990). As Oxhorn (2009, 223) writes, the economic insecurities produced by market policies "generate political apathy as people's efforts are devoted to participating in the market, and they have less time to become politically active." In turn, these outcomes jeopardize the organizational bases of representative institutions and organizations, especially political parties and labor unions (Roberts 2002, Roberts and Portes 2006). As Roberts (2002, 26–27) puts it, "Labor unions remain as political actors, but their organic ties to party and state institutions have loosened, their access to the policy making arena has narrowed, and their ability to speak for a plurality of popular interests has diminished."

A related set of arguments focuses less on the decline of civil society's mobilizing capacity, shifting attention to the ability of the postglobalization state to meet social needs after economic liberalization. Due to the powerful external constraints imposed by the institutionalization of economic reforms, some studies have argued that the postglobalization state significantly thwarts the ability of policy makers to improve the social dislocations related to economic liberalization policies. Hence social actors have little motivation to collectively organize given that the stripped-down, post-economic liberalization state no longer represents a worthy target of social mobilization. As Kurtz (2004, 271) notes, "the freeing of markets has withdrawn the government from many of its adjudicatory functions in the economy, thereby simultaneously removing a host of critical, zero-sum conflicts from the political arena itself."

In Chile and Mexico, for instance, studies have shown how economic liberalization left poor and rural segments of society disconnected from the activities of the state and without the economic or political resources needed to organize effectively against market reforms, even after democracy had taken hold (Holzner 2007; Kurtz 2004). Other studies document a decline in collective activity in Peru, including significant crackdowns on dissent, when Alberto Fujimori launched economic liberalization policies in the 1990s (Silva 2009, 244). In all of these cases economic reforms succeeded in reducing the state apparatus to a shadow of its former self, rendering it an unlikely target for protests. Consistent with the depoliticization view, in each of these cases economic liberalization created significant collective action problems and reduced incentives for large segments of the population to engage in contentious politics.

The Repoliticization Perspective

Following contributions from the literature on social movements, in particular political process theory (e.g., Tarrow 1998; Tilly and Tarrow 2006), the repoliticization perspective emphasizes the importance of national- and subnational-level political conditions as central to explaining antimarket mobilizations. These political conditions downplay the role of grievances or economic threats, such as those generated by economic liberalization, which existing literature portrays as the common source for mobilization (e.g., Silva 2009). I begin this section by outlining the main arguments of political process theory. Then I move on to explain how the focus on political conditions differs from other recent accounts of antimarket mobilizations, including the depoliticization perspective from above.

The political process model advances three analytical frameworks for studying the dynamics of protest movements: political opportunity structures, resource mobilization, and framing processes. McAdam, McCarthy, and Zald (1996) point out that these three analytical approaches are the best way to study how social movements emerge and develop. These authors suggest that social movements are initiated as a result of social changes that transform the existing political order, making it more accessible to the demands of a given social movement. When social movements perceive this opening for their demands, these changes in political conditions are subsequently transformed into opportunities. However, for a successful social movement, participants in the movement must have organizational capacity and resources available for their cause. Yet it is not enough that these social actors feel aggrieved, even if they are convinced of the potential benefits of collective action vis-à-vis other possible strategies. These actors must develop a cultural interpretive framework for their demands, and this framework needs to go beyond the specific interests of the core supporters of a movement. These frameworks attract new supporters and allow the movement to survive and succeed. In short, these three analytical approaches—political opportunity structures, resource mobilization, and framing processes—are very useful to understand the dynamics of social movements.

Political opportunities are the institutional structures or informal power relations of a given political system (e.g., Eisinger 1973; Kitschelt 1986; Brockett 1991; Tarrow 1998; Koopmans 1995). Although there is some consensus on the definition of political opportunity structures, several authors have examined different aspects of these institutional structures or informal power relations. Following McAdam (1996) and in an effort to organize this literature, the four most important dimensions of these political opportunities include: (a) the relative openness or closure of the institutionalized political system, (b) the stability or instability of elite alignments, (c) the presence or absence of elite allies, and (d) the state's capacity for repression.[4] McAdam (1996) further observes that the relevance of some of these dimensions in comparison to others should follow the research question one is posing. For example, to study the temporal and spatial variation of protest events, the formal dimensions of political opportunities, such as the relative openness of the political system, and the state's capacity for repression become the most useful dimensions to take into account (e.g., McAdam 1982; Tarrow 1998). In contrast, the informal dimensions of political opportunities, such as the stability or instability of elite alignments and the presence or absence of elite allies, have greater analytical weight if the research question focuses on the outcomes that social movements seek to achieve (e.g., Banaszak 1996; Giugni, McAdam, and Tilly 1998).

Turning to resource mobilization, the literature emphasizes the importance of preexisting mobilizing networks as essential for the existence and success of social movement organizations. Several authors dwell on the ability of social movement organizations to mobilize human and economic resources (e.g., McCarthy and Zald 1997; Piven and Cloward 1979; Cress and Snow 2000). In addition, when it comes to mobilization of marginalized or powerless groups, the collaboration of external organizers and other preexisting organizations is pivotal for the emergence of successful collective action (e.g., Jenkins and Perrow 1977; Tilly 1978).

Finally, framing processes are social constructions that act as filters or "memes" for interpreting the existing reality (e.g., Snow and Benford 1988; Benford and Snow 2000).[5] Protest movements grow because leaders frame or reframe messages in ways that can attract a larger number of sympathizers or adherents. To be clear, successful framing requires conscious strategic efforts by leaders of protest movements (Zald 1996). And generally speaking, "memes" that frame the cause of the movement in terms of injustice are more likely to be successful.

Before extending these analytical frameworks to the study of protest movements, a note on the role of grievances is warranted. Both the depoliticization and repoliticization perspectives agree that economic liberalization imposes severe material hardships on popular sectors—such as lower wages, employment insecurity, higher prices, cuts in social programs, and regressive land reform, among other examples. The question is, then, what role these grievances play in mobilizing social actors. Following the depoliticization perspective, these grievances or threats all but demobilize social actors. And the presence of political conditions as put forth by democracy is not expected to revitalize protest activity.

Other authors, in contrast, argue that these grievances or threats were pivotal for the mobilization of social actors. In Silva's (2009, 266) analysis, for instance, episodes of anti-neoliberal contention were "Polanyian backlashes to the construction of contemporary market society." And neoliberal reforms "generated the *motivation*—the grievances—for mobilization" (Silva 2009, 43, italics original).[6] Following Tilly (1978), Almeida (2007) also emphasizes the salience of negative inducements or unfavorable conditions as threats that are likely to facilitate various forms of "defensive" collective action. Harvey (2003) would characterize the claims of indigenous people in opposition to the extractive economy as "protests against dispossession." To some degree, these works mirror what political scientist James Davies called the "J-curve of rising and declining satisfactions" (Davies 1969; Davies 1962). Davies's theory suggests that protest will break out when conditions suddenly worsen and aggrieved groups seek someone to blame for the disturbing course of events. The transition to a market economy implied an erosion of social citizenship rights (e.g., access to basic social services and publicly subsidized benefits) and thus made things worse for popular sectors of civil society (Almeida 2007). Similarly, the expansion of the extractive economy entailed a greater need for water and land, and consequently, it affected both urban and rural populations.

However, and building upon political process theory (e.g., Tarrow 1998; Tilly and Tarrow 2006), the repoliticization perspective argues that an approach based solely on grievances—such as those generated by economic liberalization or the expansion of the extractive frontier—does not explain collective action very well. These grievances or threats in and of themselves seldom explain variations in the dynamics of protest movements. Thinking about resource extraction, for instance, one could easily argue that the economic history of Latin America is essentially a history of mining. Yet grievances related to resource extraction consistently outnumber outbreaks against mining, and we do not always see protest movements emerge to challenge them. Instead, political process theory focuses on the context in which a protest movement operates, or the "world outside a social movement" as Meyer (2004, 126) phrased it.

The three frameworks from political process theory—political opportunity structures, resource mobilization, and framing processes—constitute one approach to examining the broader dynamics of social movement emergence and development. The political conditions emphasized in this book capture the formal dimensions of political opportunities (the first framework from political process theory), which are useful to explain the national and subnational variation of protest movements across geography and time (e.g., McAdam 1982; Tarrow 1998). These political conditions include the moderating role of democracy, the quality of institutional representation as embodied in political parties, and finally the level of political party competition. In contrast, resource mobilization and framing processes (the other two frameworks from political process theory) are central to explaining the larger effects of protest movements on their environment. The interactivity of the three frameworks suggests that when political conditions are favorable, as in the context of democracy (political opportunities), actors can build a master frame linking economic liberalization and injustices (framing processes), which, in turn, allows for the building of broad coalitions of civil society actors (resource mobilization).

The Cross-National Variation of Protest among Countries

How does political process theory help us understand the cross-national dynamics of protest movements? In this section, and following McAdam (1996), I argue that the formal dimensions of political opportunities—that is, the relative openness of the political system as captured by the presence of democracy—explain well the temporal and spatial variation of protest events. After outlining the theoretical arguments that support this proposition, I present recent cross-national evidence that shows how political democracy aided collective responses to economic liberalization. I conclude this section by outlining the limitations of cross-national studies in providing a fully convincing account for the revival of protest under democracy, particularly in the presence of within-nation heterogeneity and complexity. It shows how research based on comparing national units easily misinterprets cases where subnational protests have had important consequences on national politics. Peru is such a case.

Following the political opportunities literature (e.g., Tilly 1978; Tarrow 1998), the repoliticization perspective focuses on the political conditions that create a favorable environment or opportunity for people to undertake collective action. At the national level, it emphasizes the systemwide or macro political opportunities advanced by democratization that are favorable for popular mobilization. As several scholars have argued, the presence of democracy enhances the opportunity for protest activity. Compared to nondemocratic regimes, democracies foster collective mobilization by relaxing repression (Francisco 2009), encouraging associational life, and opening channels of popular participation (Almeida and Johnston 2006; Almeida 2008). In this sense, democracies shape societal responses to grievances by creating "political opportunity structures" that facilitate or hinder collective mobilization (Tarrow 1998), and by and large, democratic settings "guarantee a more open political opportunity structure than their opposites" (Tilly and Tarrow 2006, 66). In autocracies, on the other hand, where political and civil rights are restricted, collective mobilizations tend to be the exception rather than the rule, as protests in these settings are "likely to invite quick (and often violent) repression" (Cook 1996, 40).

The conceptualization of democracy as an opportunity for mobilization as put forward by the repoliticization perspective also draws attention to the salience of framing processes (e.g., Snow and Benford 1988; Benford and Snow 2000; Gamson and Meyer 1996). It suggests that economic liberalization provided a strong strategic framing opportunity for the resolution of collective action problems across a diverse range of social actors, which in turn made sustained popular mobilization possible. As Roberts (2008, 330) recently noted, "market reform left unmet social needs or heightened economic insecurities that provided a basis for the collective articulation of political grievances." Economic liberalization thus produced a "master frame" (Roberts 2008, 341) for the repoliticization of popular subjects.

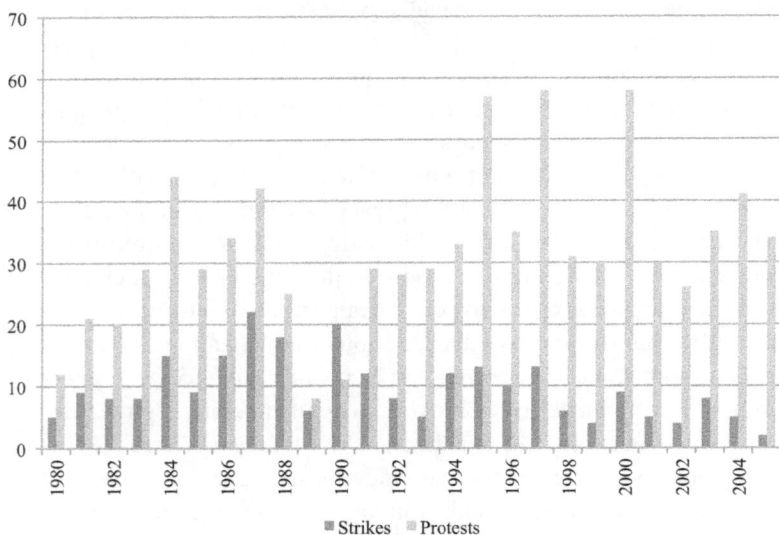

FIGURE 1. Strikes and protests in Latin America, 1980–2005. "Protests" are the number of riots and antigovernment demonstrations, capturing both nonpeaceful and peaceful contentious activity, respectively. In the Banks data, "riots" are defined as "any violent demonstration or clash of more than 100 citizens involving the use of physical force" and "anti-government demonstrations" as "any peaceful public gathering of at least 100 people for the primary purpose of displaying or voicing their opposition to government policies or authority, excluding demonstrations of a distinctly anti-foreign nature." "Strikes" are defined as "any strike of 1,000 or more industrial or service workers that involves more than one employer and that is aimed at national government policies or authority." *Source*: Banks 2010.

Recent cross-national studies are congruent with the arguments put forward by the repoliticization perspective. Using different measures of economic liberalization as well as political democracy, these large-N studies have shown that economic liberalization increases the level of contentious politics under democracy (e.g., Arce and Bellinger 2007; Arce and Kim 2011; Bellinger and Arce 2011).[7] To further illustrate the general cycle of contention surrounding economic liberalization, figure 1 compares the level of strikes with protests for the Latin American region using the Cross-National Time Series (CNTS) dataset (Banks 2010).[8] A couple of observations in support of the repoliticization perspective can be drawn from this figure. First, one can observe two waves of mobilization within this general cycle of contention. As mentioned in the introduction, the first wave corresponds to the protests against the austerity measures of the 1980s, while the second one follows the deepening of economic liberalization policies during the late 1990s, as seen in the protests against the privatization of utility services, as well as the mobilizations against the expansion of the extractive frontier as a consequence of growing volumes of foreign and domestic investments. Second, the figure also shows that in the aftermath of economic liberalization, which begins in the early 1990s for most of the region, the level of strikes decreases in comparison to that of protests. Moreover, the level of protests in the aftermath of economic liberalization is comparatively higher relative to the "lost decade" of the 1980s. Repoliticization is in full swing starting in the late 1990s and spilling over into the first decade of the 2000s.

Substantively, these cross-national studies have established a pattern of collective responses to economic liberalization under democracy that is generalizable beyond a few specific cases, thus allowing us to make broader theoretical arguments and empirical claims about the consequences of economic liberalization across the region. These cross-national studies indicate that the repoliticization effects of economic liberalization under democracy are widespread and extend beyond the four Latin American countries where protest politics appear to have been the most intense or produced large-scale political changes (e.g., the toppling of chief executives who supported market policies in Argentina, Bolivia, Ecuador, and Venezuela).

These large-N studies also bring to light the mediating role of political democracy in shaping collective responses to economic liberalization. Scholars of social movements have long argued that in the absence of a political environment that affects the incentives for people to undertake collective action (Tarrow 1998), people with intense grievances may pose only negligible challenges to existing regimes. In line with the formal dimensions of political opportunities, in general, and the repoliticization view, in particular, political democracy advanced a favorable opportunity for collective responses; in some cases it created the political space necessary for aggrieved social groups to build associational power and collective power, while in others it restrained the state's capacity for repression. Therefore, contrasting Silva's (2009) analysis, the rise of contentious activity cannot be adequately explained by emphasizing solely the grievances or economic threats that are associated with economic liberalization. At most, we can say that these grievances or threats were necessary but not sufficient conditions to set in motion episodes of anti-neoliberal contention.

More generally, the finding that political democracy aided collective responses to economic liberalization suggests that democracy following Latin America's third democratic wave is becoming gradually more meaningful, allowing collective actors to use channels outside the traditional ballot box to contest economic reform policies. It suggests that democracy in Latin America has teeth by letting popular actors modify the economic policies that challenge their lives. Collective actors in the presence of democracy, as Roberts (2008, 328) writes, "punctured the aura of inexorability that surrounded the trends toward economic liberalization and globalization in the waning decades of the twentieth century."

While the resulting body of evidence on the rise of contentious activity has shown that the general response to economic liberalization involved some form of repoliticization—not depoliticization—the emphasis on political democracy as put forth by the repoliticization perspective is only part of the larger puzzle on the consequences of economic liberalization. I conclude this section by explaining three sets of limitations from cross-national studies to provide a fully convincing account for the revival of antimarket protest under democracy.

First, the conceptualization of democracy as an opportunity for mobilization helps to explain the variation in protest across countries and over time and shows that the political opportunity for protest is generally higher in democracies than in autocracies. Yet political democracy has become increasingly more common throughout the region and continues to broaden. In the words of Kitschelt et al. (2010, 1), Latin America has grown into "the most uniformly democratic region on earth behind the established Western democracies and Japan." Therefore, given the regionwide shift to democracy, the explanatory power of democracy to understanding episodes of contention—or any other political outcome—becomes progressively less persuasive.

Second, the conceptualization of democracy as an opportunity for mobilization cannot easily explain the variation in patterns of protest across subnational boundaries, which prior research has shown to be abundant (Boulding 2010; Murillo and Ronconi 2004). In Argentina, for instance, provinces (akin to states in other countries) like Tucumán, Salta, Jujuy, and Santa Fe, which geographically occupy the country's central northeastern corridor, sustain the greatest concentration of protests compared to the remaining nineteen provinces (excluding Buenos Aires) (Arce and Mangonnet 2013). Similarly, the regions (akin to a province in Argentina) of Ayacucho, Puno, and Cusco, which are situated in the southern highlands of Peru, experience more protests than the remaining twenty regions of Peru (excluding Lima) (see chapter 2).[9] This subnational variation of protest indicates problems of generalizing about the consequences of economic liberalization on the basis on national-level aggregate data. In particular, the explanations that draw upon national-level aggregate data often overlook the high degrees of internal heterogeneity and complexity that exist within countries.

Third, this tendency to rely upon national-level aggregate data and national units of analysis runs the risk of misinterpreting important cases (Snyder 2001, 94). In Silva's (2009) analysis, for instance, Peru emerges as a divergent case that did not experience large-scale mobilizations, yet the country has seen more than its share of social protests at the subnational level (Arce 2008). Understandably, several studies take the territorial dispersion of subnational protests as a sign of the disarticulation of protest movements, and consequently, these studies underestimate the effects of subnational mobilizations on national politics. By examining the political and economic factors that shape patterns of mobilization across subnational boundaries, this book provides greater sensitivity to within-nation heterogeneity and complexity. It also offers the detailed region-by-region information on protest activity that will allow us to test many of the leading perspectives on contentious politics.

The Expansion of the Extractive Economy

The mobilizations against the expansion of the extractive economy, which are typical of the second wave of protest against economic liberalization, allow us to address several of the limitations from research based on comparing national units. As subsequent chapters elaborate, these mobilizations share similar claims (e.g., conflicts over land and water), networks of actors in opposition to mining (e.g., local communities, local mayors, regional presidents, environmental NGOs, etc.), and networks of actors in support of extraction (e.g., the mining industry, the central government, business associations and chambers of commerce, the national media, etc.), yet the trajectory of protest movements has been very dissimilar throughout the country. Up until now, case studies of protests against natural resource extraction have generated a wealth of descriptive detail, yet the main task of this book is to advance a generalized understanding of the factors that determine the dynamics of protest movements as well as their impacts.

To be clear, resource extraction has a long history throughout the developing world. In Peru, for instance, the beginnings of large-scale mining can be the traced to the operations of the Cerro de Pasco Corporation (CPC), an American mining company, at the turn of the twentieth century (chapter 3). The origins of the country's labor movement are also tied to CPC, as the company became the largest private employer in the nation. Yet the current wave of protests over natural resource extraction provides an ideal venue to understand the changing nature of mobilizations against economic liberalization as articulated by the repoliticization perspective. In particular, these mobilizations help us understand the emergence of broad coalitions with diverse sets of new actors, as well as the geographic segmentation of protest. Bebbington (2009) summarizes well the new circumstances that have arisen as a consequence of expansion of the extractive frontier (or "new mining" as other authors have called it). These changes include "the scale and pace of expansion, the financial flows involved, the domiciles and governance of the companies and finance houses investing in extraction, [and] the interaction between extraction and investment" (Bebbington 2009, 8).

Under "new mining," technological conditions have reduced the need for unskilled labor, and labor disputes between mining companies and workers have become less visible. Instead, the so-called mega extractive projects (*megaproyectos mineros*) have an increased need for water, energy, land, and landscape. New open-pit and heap-leaching techniques demand far greater access to each of these resources. These technological conditions imply that the actors involved in protests against the extraction of natural resources are largely the rural and urban populations affected by extraction. And their claims often include land, water quantity and quality, landscape, and the protection of the environment and their livelihood. Seen in this light, "new mining" allows us to understand the types of coalitions that aggrieved groups have forged in opposition to extraction, including the new actors that have emerged to challenge economic liberalization policies. These coalitions cut across classes and the urban and rural divide, as well as environmental and nationalistic discourses.

"New mining" has also surged amid favorable market conditions that are yielding remarkable profits. The price of gold, for instance, increased from US $344 in the early 1990s to US $1,225 in the late 2000s (per troy ounce). In the same period, the price of silver rose from US $4 to US $20 (per troy ounce), and the price of copper increased from US $1.03 to US $3.42 (per pound) (MEM 2010). As subsequent chapters show, the claims of groups affected by extraction also involve disputes for a better distribution of mineral rents in some cases or a revision of tax and royalty agreements between the central government and mining corporations in others. Finally, "new mining" illustrates well the geographic segmentation of mobilizations as predetermined by the location of the mines themselves. Yet as I explain later, some of these mobilizations resulted in "shifts in scale" as the agendas of local movements reached national and even international salience.

The Subnational Variation of Protest within Democratic Countries

In line with the cross-national evidence in support of repoliticization, subnationally the relationship between protest and political conditions is also closer than that between protest and economic factors. At the subnational level, and building upon Kitschelt (1986) and Almeida (2008), two interrelated political opportunities dimensions associated with democratization—political parties and political competition— allow us to examine the salience of political conditions. I begin this section by outlining the theoretical arguments that associate these conditions with the dynamics of mobilizations. Next, I discuss how contextual factors—in particular, the presence of weakly developed parties and party systems—shape the effects of these conditions on protest activity. I conclude this section by sketching the political fragmentation of parties in Peru, where already weak national parties do not win subnational offices and often do not participate in subnational elections. As chapter 3 explains, the fluidity and fragmentation of political forces in Peru epitomize the presence of poorly developed institutions, producing different effects on protest than previously theorized.

In terms of political parties, and following Kitschelt (1986), parties capture the formal dimensions of political opportunities, which again allow one to examine the variation of protest movements across geography and time (McAdam 1996). More specifically, parties are useful to examine the relative openness of the political system to the societal demands of protest movements. They are seen as points of access that influence policies, whereby the larger their number, the more open the political system is to the demands of social movements. This perspective assumes that political parties effectively articulate different demands in the electoral arena. And because of this connection, parties invite assimilative strategies; that is, protest movements attempt to work through the established political institutions as the latter offer multiple points of access (Kitschelt 1986). Ultimately, these assimilative strategies put downward pressure on the scale and intensity of mobilizations.[10]

Turning to competition, Almeida (2008) presents competitive elections as another political opportunity dimension associated with democratization. Competitive elections contribute to the formation of organizations and associations by multiple challengers and, as such, encourage the organizational growth of civil society. A competitive election "allows previously excluded groups . . . an arena in which to begin organizing drives" (Almeida 2008, 16). Therefore, competitive elections become an opportunity for mobilization. In this book, however, I redirect the analysis of political competition to the political science literature, inasmuch as it embodies one central dimension of democracy, which can also help us untangle how and why democracy affects mass mobilizations at the subnational level. Electoral theories of democracy, in fact, have long posited that political competition is the primary source of government responsiveness (e.g., Key 1966; Fiorina 1981). Through electoral rewards and punishments, political competition offers citizens the opportunity to influence the behavior of politicians and, in so doing, advances the best hope for government responsiveness. By altering the behavior of politicians, political competition also enhances the connection between public preferences and government output. Building on these arguments, several studies have shown that political competition leads to higher government responsiveness across a wide range of social outcomes, including economic performance (Przeworski and Limongi 1993), respect for human rights (Beer and Mitchell 2004), and social spending (Hecock 2006), among other things (for an expanded list, see Cleary 2010, 5). Extending these arguments to mobilizations, political competition induces greater responsiveness among politicians; therefore, when the level of underlying political competition is higher or more pronounced, politicians should be more likely to enact policies that are designed to reduce protest activity, thus increasing their popularity at election time (Arce and Rice 2009; Arce and Mangonnet 2013).[11]

However, in many new democracies contextual factors change the effects of parties and competition on protest activity. Examples of these factors include incomplete rule of law, less educated and informed electorates, clientelistic practices, shallow media systems, weak bureaucracies, endemic corruption, and poverty, among others. But chief among them is weakly developed parties and party systems. In many young democracies, parties do not appropriately articulate societal demands and, as such, do not provide adequate points of access to shape policy, irrespective of their number or proximity to voters as a consequence of the creation of subnational governments, as in Peru in the early 2000s (chapter 3). Rather than inviting assimilative strategies, in these settings movements engage in confrontational, disruptive strategies outside established policy channels. This argument is also supported by research that has shown that countries with weak institutions breed a higher tendency to use protest as an instrument to influence those who govern (Arce 2010b; Machado, Scartascini, and Tommasi 2009).

In many new democracies, weakly developed parties and party systems also impair the mechanisms of responsiveness and accountability that are typically associated with political competition and thus strain the connection between public preferences and government output. Stated differently, in these settings political competition fails to enhance policy responsiveness, and hence competition is less likely to reduce protest activity. The implication here is that the mechanisms of responsiveness and accountability that are tied to political competition vary according to the context where competition takes place. Therefore, rather than assuming that the connection between competition and responsiveness always functions smoothly in any given case, the effects of competition on protest need more careful scrutiny.

Peru provides an ideal setting to examine the salience of subnational political conditions on protest in the presence of weak institutions. The country's party system has been plagued by political outsiders since 1990; Fujimori, Toledo, and Humala were political novices who presided over disposable, candidate-centered parties (Levitsky and Cameron 2003). Peruvian political parties are thus weak and deeply fragmented entities (chapter 2), and, as such, the number of political parties does not work well to gauge the openness of the polity. Moreover, the government of Toledo advanced new outlets for political representation at the subnational level known as "regions" (chapter 3), and these new outlets, by virtue of their proximity to local conditions, could have in principle boosted the connection between public preferences and government output. However, the country's already weak national parties have been incapable of successfully competing in subnational elections; thus different levels of government have developed their own political and electoral movements. Across several regional elections, amateur politicians elected with fragile pluralities, and without ties to national-level organizations, have made up the bulk of regional governments. Therefore, it is likely that the country's fragmentation of political forces may have strained the mechanisms of responsiveness and accountability that are typically associated with political competition. Thus, while subnational elections are highly competitive, political competition does not enhance government or policy responsiveness; rather, it is associated with higher levels of subnational protest (chapter 3).

Up to this point, I have primarily discussed political opportunities—the first framework from political process theory—in the context of the social movement literature. Specifically, I have emphasized the notion of democracy as an opportunity for mobilization to explain the national variation of protests across countries. I have also presented two formal political opportunities dimensions associated with democratization—political parties and political competition—that are helpful to examine the subnational variation of protest within democracies. Although each captures different elements of democracy (e.g., parties that provide points of access in policy making and competition that encourages policy responsiveness), both are ultimately interconnected. I also explained how contextual factors, in particular the presence of poorly developed institutions, may produce different effects on mobilizations than previously anticipated. The final section of this chapter redirects attention to the effects of mobilizations on the trajectory of the state.

The Impact of Protest Movements on Their Environment

The last question posed in this chapter is: Under what conditions are protest movements, which initially appear to be localized, segmented outbursts, likely to produce substantive gains for aggrieved groups (i.e., changes of policy in response to protest)? The mobilizations against the expansion of the extractive frontier, which again are typical of the second wave of protests against economic liberalization and are presented in the second half of this book, highlight the importance of resource mobilization as well as framing processes—the other two frameworks from political process theory.

As chapters 4, 5, and 6 explain, one way to understand the outcomes of the hundreds of protests against resource extraction is by taking into account the relative economic importance of mining compared to other economic activities—in particular agriculture—as well as the relative strength of aggrieved groups compared to those in support of mining interests (see table 1). In several regions of Peru, particularly in the central highlands, mining is not in competition with agriculture and, as a consequence, represents the only opportunity for making a living. The region of Pasco, situated at 4,380 meters (14,370 feet) above sea level, is a good example. As noted in chapter 3, the beginnings of large-scale mining in Peru can be traced to this location, and despite the presence of important mobilizations then and now, resource extraction continues unaffected. To diffuse the demands from protestors, mining companies often provide selective material rewards to the leaders of protest organizations (e.g., bribes, employment opportunities, etc.) or spend money on high-profile projects in collaboration with local authorities, mostly municipal mayors (e.g., the beautification of the town's central plaza, the rebuilding of the town's school, etc.). The goal is to win the support of the local population and authorities through a series of small concessions. Mining companies also collude with the local media (e.g., the local newspaper and radio station) to harass and intimidate the leaders of protest movements, including the NGOs that oppose mining.

TABLE 1. Typology of protest outcomes

Collective Action	Competition with Agriculture	
	Low	High
Low	Extraction deepens Sporadic mobilizations	Extraction stops and goes Sporadic mobilizations Example: Mount Quilish
High	Extraction stops and goes Sustained mobilizations Example: Bagua	Extraction stalls Sustained mobilizations Example: Tambogrande

In cases where mining competes with agriculture, as in Tambogrande (chapter 4) and Mount Quilish (chapter 5), the agricultural economy, by its very definition, makes available a range of preexisting organizations, such as producers' associations (*asociaciones de productores*) and water users' boards (*junta de usuarios de riego*), through which sustained mobilizations can develop. In both Tambogrande and Mount Quilish, these agriculture-based organizations quickly coalesced into larger opposition movements known as defense fronts (*frentes de defensa*). Moreover, in other protests against the expansion of the extractive economy, the participation of Oxfam and other NGOs was crucial for the coordination of collective action among aggrieved communities affected by mining (Arce 2008, 52–55).[12] These agriculture-based organizations as well as NGOs exemplify the importance of resource mobilization for the emergence of successful collective action. Yet the outcome of mobilizations where mining and agriculture are in competition with each other ultimately hinges on the relative strength of aggrieved groups vis-à-vis mining interests. Specifically, the strength of opposition groups is shaped by their associational power and their collective power. Associational power (or organizational capacity) refers to the ability of subordinate social groups to create new organizations or recast existing ones (e.g., transforming an agriculture-based organization into a defense front). Collective power (or coalitional capacity) refers to the ability of subordinate social groups to forge coalitions across new or recast organizations (e.g., forming a coalition between a defense front and other organizations outside the region affected by extraction).[13] Generally, low collective action implies weak associational power and weak collective power. High collective action implies the opposite (see table 1). As subsequent chapters demonstrate, strategic framing was instrumental for aggrieved groups to build associational power, as well as collective power.

In Tambogrande, local leaders opposed to mining had strong ties to local organizations and established a network of support consisting of national and international NGOs that successfully connected the antimining mobilization to the country's national identity. Tambogrande is lime rich, and limes are a key ingredient in a number of traditional Peruvian dishes. What is more, the presence of organizations with strong ties to the local community served as a check on leaders and made the possible distribution of material rewards or other forms of cooptation ineffective. Conversely, local leaders had a better grip on organizations and engaged in effective resistance, mixing what could be initially characterized as confrontational, disruptive strategies (e.g., burning the machinery of Manhattan Minerals Corporation) with assimilative, more traditional types of grassroots democracy (e.g., referendum).

In contrast, in the northern region of Cajamarca, the Yanacocha mine has been subject to sporadic protests due to environmental contamination, land use matters, water rights disputes, and so on. However, the organizations opposed to mining are highly fragmented and generally have not developed a larger network of support beyond the region itself. Thus their fragmentation did not evolve into a process known as "scale-shift" (McAdam, Tarrow, and Tilly 2001), in which isolated instances of protests transform into growing streams of mobilization. In several of these protests, aggrieved groups and the Yanacocha mine agreed to negotiate their differences by establishing a bargaining roundtable (*mesa de diálogo*) and then settled by signing a deed of commitment (*acta de compromiso*). Mining operations may be interrupted while negotiations take place but later resume once a settlement has been reached. An important exception from this stop-and-go pattern was the mobilization of Mount Quilish (chapter 5), where thousands of protestors staged a two-week general strike and derailed the expansion of the Yanacocha mine, albeit momentarily.

Finally, the mobilization in opposition to the opening of the Amazon for development in Bagua in 2009 was not directly tied to agriculture, as in the previous cases of Tambogrande and Mount Quilish. Rather, it had to do more with the potential for deforestation as a consequence of logging and oil exploration by transnational corporations. In this region, aggrieved groups were already organized in AIDESEP (Interethnic Development Association of the Peruvian Rainforest), an ethnic indigenous federation that has existed for decades. AIDESEP's ability to mount an effective resistance rests on the cultural identity of the peoples who have inhabited the Amazon for generations. AIDESEP is also part of a larger network of similar indigenous organizations in Ecuador and Bolivia. Resource extraction continues in the Amazon region but has been limited in scale as a result of AIDESEP's actions.

The protests where competition with agriculture is low and collective action is also low typically comprise the "demands for services" category of mobilizations described in chapter 3. These mobilizations seek a better distribution of the town's mineral wealth and are not necessarily antimining. The other cases represented in table 1 follow the "demand for rights" category of mobilizations. These mobilizations are against resource extraction and are motivated by environmental concerns in defense of the water supply or the protection of agricultural lands. As subsequent chapters show, only the latter category of mobilizations has had important national policy effects.

The dual transition toward economic liberalization and democracy has puzzled scholars for several decades as research has sought to understand how these complex phenomena complement or contradict one another. The depoliticization perspective views free markets and democracy as incompatible with each other, arguing that the forces of economic liberalization are inexorable and thus continue to move forward at the expense of democracy. Building on political process theory (e.g., Tarrow 1998; Tilly and Tarrow 2006), the repoliticization perspective, in contrast, underlines the importance of political conditions—democracy—in creating a favorable environment to address the grievances or threats caused by economic liberalization. Thus democratic contexts enhance the opportunity for protest activity. As summarized in this chapter, the Latin American experience is more closely aligned with the repoliticization perspective (e.g., Arce and Bellinger 2007; Arce and Kim 2011; Bellinger and Arce 2011).

By emphasizing the importance of democracy as a mediating variable affecting the relationship between economic liberalization and protest activity, the book shifts attention toward the salience of political conditions in an area of research that has traditionally dwelled on the structural influence of economic factors or conditions. Until recently, in fact, economic liberalization and globalization were thought to prefigure "the end of politics," eclipsing national governments and their sovereignty. The book's conceptualization of democracy as an opportunity for mobilization, in contrast, suggests that democracy following Latin America's third democratic wave is becoming gradually more meaningful, allowing collective actors to use channels outside the traditional ballot box to contest or modify the economic reform policies that challenge their lives.

The book's emphasis on the effects of political competition sums up a central attribute of a multidimensional concept, such as democracy. It allows us to examine the salience of political conditions at the subnational level and further see how competition can generate very different effects depending on the institutional setting in which it takes place. The presence of poorly developed institutions, in particular, is likely to damage the mechanisms of responsiveness and accountability that are often linked to political competition and thus strain the connection between public preferences and government output. What is more, given the fluidity of political institutions in Peru, the focus on political competition is theoretically stronger than an analysis based on the number of parties that participate in subnational elections. At most, we can say that subnational parties do not invite assimilative strategies for protest movements. On balance, the book's new take on protest—subnational political competition—sheds light on a broader theme—democracy—and builds on earlier work that has shown that greater levels of political competition are associated with lower levels of subnational protest in Argentina (Arce and Mangonnet 2013) and Bolivia (Arce and Rice 2009).

Returning to political process theory, chapters 2 and 3 emphasize the formal dimensions of political opportunities to explain the variation of protest events across time and space. In contrast, the comparative analysis presented in chapters 4, 5, and 6 draws attention to resource mobilization and framing processes to examine the larger impact of protest movements on their environment. These three frameworks—political opportunity, resource mobilization, and the framing process—dominate the social movement literature (McAdam, McCarthy, and Zald 1996, 7) and represent a unified approach to understanding the broader dynamics of protest movement emergence and development (Piven and Cloward 1979; McAdam 1982). Thus in the presence of favorable political conditions, as in the context of democracy (political opportunities), societal actors can build a master frame linking resource extraction and injustices (framing processes), which, in turn, allows for the building of broad coalitions with diverse sets of actors (resource mobilization).

CHAPTER 2

WAVES OF CONTENTIOUS POLITICS IN PERU

Several studies on the recent surge of mobilizations in Peru emphasize three broad characteristics of contentious episodes: their geographical segmentation or dispersion throughout the country; the presence of weak organizations supporting protest activity; and, finally, their low influence on national politics given the localized nature of the demands or policy goals of protest groups.[1] Generally, these mobilizations did not produce a "scale-shift" (McAdam, Tarrow, and Tilly 2001), that is, a process in which isolated instances of protests transform into national-level protest movements. These studies also make note of the eruption of protests in a context of unprecedented economic expansion, aided by soaring commodity prices and the growing Chinese demand for raw materials. The bulk of these works, however, focuses largely on the contemporary period, to be more precise, after 2004, which is when the Peruvian Office of the Ombudsman (Defensoría del Pueblo) began to track the presence of social protests across the country. Consequently, this literature emphasizes short-term contextual factors, which can be misleading indicators of the causes of long-term protest activity.

This chapter widens the time horizon on the study of contentious activity in Peru, starting with the country's transition to democracy in 1980 until 2010. It draws on an original protest event dataset recording thirty-one years of mobilizations based on the Peruvian print media to explain the long-term political and economic factors that have shaped mobilization and demobilization trends in the country under democracy. The first part of this chapter provides relevant background information centered on the commonly used arguments made to explain protest trends in Peru. These arguments include the state of the economy and the presence of political violence. The second section of this chapter utilizes the protest event dataset to reexamine these arguments, as well as other conjectures formulated to explain mobilization and demobilization trends across the Latin American region. In congruence with this book's emphasis on political conditions, following contributions from political process theory (Tarrow 1998; Tilly and Tarrow 2006), the broader political environment in which protest emerges provides a better explanation for the dynamics of protest movements over the three decades under study.

Peru under Democracy

During the 1980s, following the country's transition to democracy, Peruvian party politics appeared relatively stable: four major parties— the center-right Popular Action (AP), the American Popular Revolutionary Alliance (APRA), the leftist United Left (IU) and the conservative Popular Christian Party (PPC)—accounted for the bulk of the popular vote (Dietz and Myers 2007, 69; Levitsky 1999). These parties possessed national structures, discernible programs or ideologies, and identifiable social bases (Levitsky and Cameron 2003, 6). The 1980s, however, were also a period of economic upheaval, marked by rising inflation, declining real wages, widespread unemployment, and the resulting informalization of the workforce. GDP dropped about 25 percent in the late 1980s, and annual inflation reached a historic record of 7,649 percent in 1990. Moreover, the emergence of guerrilla groups, such as the Shining Path (Sendero Luminoso) and the MRTA (Tupac Amaru Revolutionary Movement) posed a serious threat to civilian rule (see McClintock 1998; Palmer 1992).

The economic collapse and heightened levels of political violence of the 1980s led to the implosion of the established parties of that decade. The growth of the informal economy, which represented more than 50 percent of the economically active population by 1990, further weakened class-based organizations and eliminated partisan identities among organized workers (Cameron 1994). Alberto Fujimori, a reform-minded politician, capitalized on these economic and social hardships and won the presidency in August 1990. In the 1995 presidential election, which resulted in Fujimori's second consecutive pres-

TABLE 2. Average indicators by decade in Peru

	1980–89	1990–99	2000–2010
Economy			
GDP growth	0.65	3.24	5.46
GDP per capita growth	−3.20	2.10	4.40
GDP mining growth	0.94	6.19	5.06
Inflation	528	794	2
Political Violence			
Deaths by the Shining Path	785	428	na
Deaths by the military	515	192	na
Disappearances	233	94	na
Tortures	360	258	na
Extrajudicial killings	1,431	745	na
Contentious Activity			
Strikes	267	38	64
Protests	99	118	294

Sources: Economic indicators were taken from Banco Central de Reserva del Perú 2012. Political violence indicators were taken from Comisión de la Verdad y Reconciliación 2003.

Note: Political violence average indicators for the period 1990–99 also include the year 2000. Contentious activity figures were taken from the Base de Protestas Sociales del Perú (Arce 2014; also see the appendix). Protests are the sum of mobilizations, roadblocks, sit-ins, and takeovers. These types of protest events collectively capture the repoliticization effects of economic liberalization discussed in earlier chapters.

idential term, the major political parties of the 1980s (AP, APRA, PPC, and IU) collectively accounted for only 10 percent of the popular vote (Dietz and Myers 2007, 69).

As has been amply documented elsewhere (e.g., Cameron and Mauceri 1997; Carrión 2006; Conaghan 2005; Arce 2005; Weyland 2002), Fujimori was a political outsider who successfully stabilized the economy by implementing market-oriented economic policies. GDP grew on average by 3.24 percent throughout the 1990s, and annual inflation dropped to single digits beginning in 1997. These market policies continued and expanded into the next decade under different democratically elected governments. Fujimori also controlled rampant political violence by engaging in selective repression and unleashing the military and intelligence service to defeat the ongoing insurgency (Obando 1998) (see table 2). By many different accounts, Fujimori was a very popular—albeit authoritarian and corrupt—president. The swift dissolution of Congress in the "self-coup" of April 1992 and the mass firing of judges and prosecutors exemplify well the authoritarian tendencies of the Fujimori regime (Mauceri 1995).

Fujimori ran for (and won) reelection for a third consecutive term that began in July 2000, but mounting evidence of corruption and gross criminality forced him to resign from office in November of that same year. Mass mobilizations against Fujimori began as early as 1997, when Fujimori's party voted to dismiss three members of the Constitutional Tribunal (Tribunal Constitucional, TC) who had ruled that Fujimori could not seek a third term as president, and escalated around the presidential elections of 2000 over allegations of electoral fraud. After Fujimori's abrupt resignation, Valentín Paniagua was elected president of Peru's unicameral Congress and appointed as a caretaker president of the country. Paniagua set up the National Truth Commission to investigate the human rights abuses that took place during the country's two-decade-long insurgency war. Conflict with insurgency groups had left a death toll of more than sixty-nine thousand people, among them civilians, armed forces, and insurgent militants. The violence disproportionately affected those living in remote regions where the Shining Path had strategically sought to establish its stronghold: about two-thirds of the people who were killed or disappeared spoke Quechua, one of the country's most widely spoken indigenous languages (Comisión de la Verdad y Reconciliación 2003). Paniagua called for new presidential elections to be held in April 2001.

The Post-Fujimori Era

Starting with the government of Toledo (2001–6) and continuing with the second government of APRA's Alan García (2006–11), collective protests surged and became a common mechanism to obtain political objectives or express policy demands. The episodes of contention of the first decade of the 2000s took place in a context where the threat of guerrilla insurgency had all but disappeared, where politics had become more liberalized, and with a livelier and freer press following the end of the Fujimori regime. The 2000s also provided increasing opportunities for political participation, namely the creation of regional governments, which unfolded under a remarkable period of economic expansion.

On the political scene, the government of Alejandro Toledo (2001–6) began an important process of decentralization (McNulty 2011). The decentralization initiative called for the election of twenty-five regional governments starting in November 2002. Each of these regions elected a president. The regional authorities were set up to complement the preexisting government structure, which involved twenty-four departments, 195 provinces, and 1,828 districts. Among the provinces, the port city of Callao enjoyed special status because of its economic importance. Thus, the decentralization initiative provided for political representation at the departmental level, as well as in Callao. Regional presidents, rather than the national government, were to be directly involved in the economic development of their regions by supervising infrastructure and other investment projects. These intermediate governments, as Eduardo Ballón (2011, 196) points out, "have evolved slowly, not only as counterpoints to the national government in the struggle over the distribution of resources, but also in defining the orientation of some public policies."

Toledo's reforms sought to reverse long-standing patterns of economic and political centralization in the country. This centralization made the coastal capital city of Lima the main epicenter of economic activity, as well as political control, and has historically cleaved the capital with the highlands of the country. Or, as Peruvian historian Jorge Basadre (1978) phrases it, it produced "two Perus": the "official Peru" ("Perú oficial"), located in Lima, where the bureaucracy was seated, and the "deep Peru" ("Perú profundo"), where indigenous people lived. Toledo's reforms were also aimed to undo the centralized control under Fujimori.[2] Before Toledo's reforms, in fact, the most recent decentralizing initiative took place under the first government of Alan García (1985–90). In the late 1980s, the government of García provided for the creation of thirteen regions. However, these subnational governments were quickly dismantled by the Fujimori regime following the 1992 *autogolpe*, or "self-coup," in which Fujimori dissolved the national legislature and reorganized the judiciary, thus suspending democratic and constitutional rule.[3]

The regional elections of 2002, 2006, and 2010, following Toledo's decentralization initiative, reflected the continuing fragmentation of

Peru's party system. In the elections of 2002, for instance, Toledo's party, Perú Posible, won only one regional government: Callao.[4] The bulk of the regional presidencies were won by APRA (twelve regions) and independent movements (eight regions). Yet APRA's electoral gains were also short-lived. In the elections of 2006, APRA's control was reduced to two regions: La Libertad and Piura. In the elections of 2010, APRA, which remains the only national party that consistently participates at the subnational level, retained only one regional presidency (La Libertad). The 2006 and 2010 elections, in particular, witnessed the rapid incursion of several independent parties or regional movements (*movimientos regionales*). In the 2006 elections, they won twenty-one regional presidencies, and in the 2010 election, they controlled nineteen. Reviewing the participation of parties in the regional elections of 2002, 2006, and 2010, Vergara (2011, 78) writes: "National parties are confined to the national level of government having all but given up subnational competition." Commenting on the 2010 regional elections, Levitsky (2013, 295) notes that the "emerging regional movements were as loosely organized, personalistic, and ephemeral as the parties they replaced." In most cases, as addressed in subsequent chapters, the interests of national- and regional-level politicians were in opposition. And regional politicians have encouraged the use of protest to achieve political goals or articulate policy demands.

With respect to economic policy, the governments of Toledo and García have embraced and deepened the economic liberalization policies that were set in place by Fujimori. This policy continuity, which spreads over more than two decades, departs from the policy pendulum of the 1970s and 1980s that favored protectionism in some years and liberalization in others. What's more, Toledo was instrumental in starting the negotiations for a free trade agreement with the United States. The agreement was signed on April 12, 2006, and entered into force on February 1, 2009. García also sponsored free trade agreements with other countries, such as China, Chile, Canada, and South Korea. Peru now has more than a dozen of these free trade agreements with other countries and trading blocks, including the European Union and MERCOSUR (Southern Common Market). While some of these agreements are underutilized, they have nonetheless made trade liberalization the country's de facto state policy and thus cemented the market reforms from the Fujimori decade.

In terms of economic performance, Peru has become one of the fastest-growing and most stable economies in the region. In 2005 and 2006, for instance, the country's GDP grew by 6.8 and 7.7 percent, respectively. In 2008, the Peruvian economy rose by 9.8 percent—turning the country into one of the best-performing economies in the Latin American region (BCRP 2012, 16). From July 2001 until March 2009, the economy accumulated ninety-three months of continuous growth. This process of expansion was briefly slowed down by the US financial crisis of 2008–9 but later resumed toward the end of 2009. Since October 2009 until late 2013, monthly economic growth remains strong and resilient. Similarly, GDP per capita more than doubled between 1990 (the start of the Fujimori era) and 2012 (from 3,791 to 7,916 Peruvian soles based on constant soles of 1994) (BCRP 2012, 239). The percentage of the population living in poverty also declined, from 58.7 percent in 2004 to 27.8 percent in 2011, and the percentage of the population living in extreme poverty dropped from 16.4 percent in 2004 to 6.3 percent in 2011 (BCRP 2012, 46). A growing, consumer-oriented middle class has emerged from this economic expansion. In 2013, the World Bank characterized the growth of the Peruvian economy as "Asian" because it mirrored the growth rates of East Asian economies.[5] However, not all Peruvians shared in the benefits of this economic expansion, and this uneven growth affected a number of important electoral contests.

As one would expect, the return of APRA's Alan García, the president mostly responsible for the economic collapse and heightened insurgent violence of the 1980s, surprised many observers. García began his second mandate with demands for social inclusion and equitable growth to better integrate the country (Cameron 2011a, 375). These calls were in response to the presidential results of 2006, which revealed an important schism between Lima and the northern coastal areas of the country, versus the south and central highlands of Peru. In the 2006 presidential elections, Lima and the coastal areas supported García. In contrast, the south and central highlands of Peru, including the Amazon region, voted overwhelmingly in favor of Ollanta Humala, a nationalist and founder of the Nationalist Party of Peru (PNP), who ultimately lost to García in the runoff election.

This polarization also resurfaced in the presidential elections of 2011. Lima and the coastal areas supported Keiko Fujimori (daughter of former president Alberto Fujimori). The south and central high-lands of Peru, including the Amazon region, again voted overwhelm-ingly in favor of Ollanta Humala, who defeated Keiko Fujimori in the runoff election and became the current president of the country for the period 2011–16. Gana Perú (Peru Wins) was Ollanta's party for this election. This schism showed that the market reforms that began with Fujimori generally did well in Lima and the coastal territories, yet the benefits failed to reach the south and central highlands of the country (Arce 2008, 48–49; Cotler 2011, 548).[6] This polarization reaffirmed the long-standing divide between the coastal capital of Lima and the highlands of the country alluded to earlier. Thus "two Perus" resur-faced from perceptions of inclusion and exclusion. Where growth was visible, this created a feeling of social inclusion. And where growth was lacking, many felt excluded from prosperity.

Making note of the polarization in the 2006 presidential elections, Cameron (2011a, 375) argues that García chose not to pay attention to the voters who rejected him in favor of Humala. García told journal-ists that he would not "Humalize" himself ("no me voy a humalizar"), declaring: "My first commitment is to my program and my electorate." This was an about-face change from the slogan of García's first govern-ment (1985–90), which read: "My commitment is to all Peruvians." The outcome of García's political strategy was greater social exclusion and marginalization among urban and rural labor, and even the middle classes, particularly outside Lima and the northern coastal areas of the country. In Silva's (2009, 29) study of contentious episodes in the Latin American region, social exclusion among labor and the middle classes was a "powerful force behind the unification of streams of anti-neoliberal mobilization." However, the key distinction between Peru and the other Latin American countries is that this social exclusion unfolded in the context of an economic boom that placed the country's performance at the top of the Latin American region. In contrast, in other Latin American countries antimarket protests were magnified by the presence of a protracted economic crisis.

With rising mobilizations, Toledo and García were both caught between a rock and a hard place. On the one hand, both were keen on sustaining the country's growth by expanding the extractive economy and endorsing other economic initiatives, like free trade agreements. Achieving these goals required bolstering the confidence of foreign and domestic investors, and widespread protests counteracted their efforts to improve the country's investment climate. On the other hand, they had to address the social unrest at some level. Siding with protestors too quickly could shatter business confidence, but waiting too long to respond to the protestors' demands could potentially produce violence and thus backfire politically, as in the case of Bagua (chapter 6).

Some authors suggest that the failure of Toledo and García to face the social unrest was simply a by-product of weak state capacity (Thorp 2012; De Echave et al. 2009). Other authors take note of their governments' passive response to mobilizations, interpreting this passiveness in two ways. The first way assumes that both Toledo and García anticipated that economic growth would eventually trickle down to the rest of the country, which up until then had mostly favored the coastal areas, including Lima, but left the highlands behind. This explanation suggests that they were simply waiting for this to occur, thus deeming intervention unnecessary. The other way posits that they anticipated that the newly created regional governments would step up to resolve these protests; however, as subsequent chapters document, some regional authorities actively encouraged mobilizations in opposition to both mining companies and the central government's support for extractive activities. Despite their apparent passiveness, it is worth noting that two separate government agencies kept a close watch on the evolution of these mobilizations, particularly those against resource extraction: the Office of the Ombudsman (Defensoría del Pueblo) and the Ministry of the Interior (Ministerio del Interior) (Arce 2010a). From that, we can assume that their governments were cognizant of these mobilizations, even if this knowledge did not lead to immediate action.

An alternative way to understand their governments' response to rising mobilizations is by alluding to what Peruvian novelist and Nobel laureate Mario Vargas Llosa called the "art of rocking" ("el arte de mecer").[7] In his words, "rocking is keeping a person in uncertainty and deception for a long time, but in a friendly and even affectionate way." It is "a widespread practice in Peru, a national sport," the novelist adds. As the case studies from this book demonstrate, it equates to making protestors believe the answer to their claims is a "yes" when it is, in fact, a "no." Toledo and García, for instance, would string along protestors by creating bargaining roundtables (*mesas de diálogo*) for the purposes of negotiating the latter's claims. The creation of mesas raised protestors' hopes that a solution was attainable and in tandem showed that the government was interested in the grievances of the towns affected by extraction. Yet on balance, these roundtables routinely promised more than they could deliver and failed to produce politically binding commitments.

"Rocking" worked in the government's favor for at least two reasons. First, as the social movement literature reminds us, large-scale mobilizations are difficult to sustain over a long period of time. Protests, in fact, require a lot of organization and mobilization of resources. They also require that participants devote time outside of their daily routines to sustain them. Thus, the longer their governments strung protestors along, the more likely that the protests would die down, given the difficulties of sustaining a mobilization. Second, the geographic dispersion of protests and the fragmentation of protest organizations made rising mobilizations less visible nationally, at least in the short term. These circumstances gave Toledo and García some breathing space and minimized the urgency of action.

Overall, it is not immediately apparent that Toledo and García had a clear strategy to deal with rising protests. This is why several observers have criticized their passive response to mobilizations, if they made any response at all. "Rocked" is how aggrieved groups felt, and regardless of whether it was intentional or not, it allowed their governments to continue promoting the country's investment climate amid rising protests.

Similarities notwithstanding, there are a few important differences that set Toledo apart from García. By 2001, Toledo had become the country's first popularly elected president of Andean roots, and while in office, he effectively politicized indigenous issues and made numerous overt attempts to court indigenous voters.[8] While his government failed to address the plight of indigenous groups, particularly regarding environmental damage to indigenous habitats and the dislocations that resulted from the concessions given to mining companies (Greene 2006), his political discourse remained largely pro-indigenous and nonrepressive (Paredes 2011). García, in contrast, was willing to use the repressive apparatus of the state to confront indigenous mobilizations. During the mobilization in opposition to the opening of the Amazon for development in Bagua (chapter 6), thirty-three people were killed when the police and the military were deployed to crack down on demonstrators. The protest gained international attention when the *Economist* reported these events in an article entitled "Blood in the Jungle."[9] Many observers also concur that García's response to rising mobilizations was anti-indigenous, even racist. Addressing the demands of indigenous people in the Amazon, García stated: "Enough is enough. These people are not monarchy, they are not first-class citizens. Who are 400,000 natives to tell 28 million Peruvians that you have no right to come here? This is a grave error, and whoever thinks this way wants to lead us to irrationality and a retrograde primitivism" (quoted in Cameron 2011a, 394).

Up until now, the preceding narrative on Peru has touched upon some of the general arguments made to explain mobilization and demobilization trends introduced in chapter 1. For instance, in terms of a grievance-centered approach that emphasizes economic conditions, economic growth in Peru was restored in the mid-1990s and continues in the present period. The average growth for the decade of the 1980s was 0.65 percent of GDP, increasing to 3.24 percent in the 1990s and later to 5.64 percent in the 2000s. The levels of political violence and repression were also higher in the 1980s compared to later decades (see table 2). More important, democracy bounced back after the Fujimori decade and provided new outlets for political representation at the regional level. The next section draws upon an original protest event dataset recording thirty-one years of mobilizations to reevaluate these arguments as well as other conjectures formulated to explain mobilization and demobilization trends across the Latin American region.

Common Explanations of Protest Trends in Peru

Two broad waves of protest can be observed since Peru's transition to democracy in 1980: one during the early to mid-1980s and the other one in the mid- to late 2000s (see figure 2). These two waves surfaced under starkly different sociopolitical and economic conditions. The 1980s were a period of economic decline and increasing political violence. The 2000s, in contrast, were a period of economic expansion taking place in a context of overall pacification. The level of political liberalization was comparatively similar across the 1980s and 2000s and also higher than that of the 1990s—the Fujimori decade.[10] The analysis presented here casts doubt on two commonly used arguments formulated to explain protest trends in Peru. These explanations include the state of the economy and the presence of political violence.

Turning to the economy, the conventional wisdom suggests that crisis conditions emboldened popular sectors and middle classes to mobilize (Silva 2009). The first wave of protest of the 1980s is consistent with this argument. The 1980s were a period of economic upheaval, and those mobilizations largely followed the "bad news" of the economy, for example, higher consumer prices due to inflation, food shortages, and poor provision of basic government services. The second wave of protest of the 2000s, however, defies the conventional wisdom that associates lackluster economic performance with greater levels of mobilizations. In the 2000s, the Peruvian economy rebounded and became a showcase of economic stewardship. These mobilizations trailed the "good news" of economic expansion and improved performance, for example, higher wages, more benefits, and better provision of social services.[11] President García (2006–11) characterized these protests as mobilizations "originated by the abundance" of natural resources (quoted in Meléndez and León 2009, 606). Overall, the finding that protests are linked to the state of the economy when it is doing poorly (the 1980s) or well (the 2000s) suggests that national-level economic conditions are generally not a good predictor of mobilization and demobilization trends in the country.[12] At the least, the evidence suggests that the relationship between the state of the economy and protest is more complex than it appears. For this reason, it is imperative to pin down the sources of grievances linked to the state of the economy, especially at the subnational level. Subsequent chapters do so by looking at one particular set of mobilizations that are tied to a specific type of economic policy: natural resource extraction.

Turning to the political violence argument, several scholars have argued that the country's insurgency war made it difficult for social groups to build associational power and collective power, which had been crucial in resisting economic liberalization policies elsewhere (Arellano-Yanguas 2008; Silva 2009). The Shining Path, in particular, targeted and assassinated several leaders of grassroots organizations because these leaders were viewed as supportive of the existing political apparatus, instead of the insurgency (I return to this point in the conclusion). A related set of arguments associates state repression as a result of political violence with the decline of mobilizations. In brief, if political violence quells mobilizations due to deaths or repressive activities, one would expect lower levels of mobilizations when violence is generally high. However, as table 2 shows, violence and protests coexisted during the 1980s; thus it is not immediately clear whether political violence made the presence of antigovernment mobilizations unlikely. The information about political violence comes from the National Truth Commission (renamed the National Truth and Reconciliation Commission under Toledo) and covers the period of the country's insurgency war, starting in 1980 until 2000. In addition, the arguments about state repression center mostly on Fujimori, given his extensive use of military intelligence and selective repression to halt the country's insurgency war. However, according to the Physical Integrity Rights Index (Cingranelli and Richards 2010), which is a composite indicator measuring tortures, extrajudicial killings, political imprisonments, and disappearances, the worst period of human rights violations in Peru was the late 1980s under the first government of García, not the 1990s under Fujimori. To summarize, the argument that political violence discouraged protest activity is not entirely satisfactory, because high levels of political violence and protest overlapped considerably during the 1980s.

In summary, the longer time horizon captured by the Peruvian protest event dataset unveils two broad waves of protest, and these waves cast doubt on the salience of two commonly used explanations of protest trends in the country, as the arguments about the state of the economy and the presence of political violence are validated in some periods and not others. These findings reaffirm the need to look beyond short-term contextual factors, which can be misleading indicators of the causes of long-term protest activity.

Democracy as an Opportunity for Repoliticization

To recast the central argument of this book, political conditions provide a better explanation to understand the dynamics of protest movements. The salience of these political conditions comes from the contributions of political process theory (Tarrow 1998; Tilly and Tarrow 2006), in particular the formal dimensions of political opportunities, which again allow one to examine the variation of protest movements across geography and time (McAdam 1996). Consistent with these arguments, figure 2 shows that the level of democracy in Peru is closely tied to the two different waves of popular contention referenced above. In fact, since the country's transition to democracy in mid-1980, Peru's level of democracy has approximated an N-shaped curve: higher in the 1980s, lower in the 1990s, and higher again in the 2000s. Echoing this observation, Freedom House scores for political rights and civil liberties classified Peru as "free" in the 1980s, "partly free" in the 1990s, and "free" in the 2000s.[13] With respect to mobilizations, again their level was also higher during the "free" periods of the 1980s and 2000s compared to the "partly free" period of the 1990s. The information supports the general idea that democracy provides a favorable environment to undertake collective action, producing distinct waves and modes of popular contention. Hence, democracy became an opportunity for the repoliticization of popular subjects. Peru's current wave of protest (the mid- to late 2000s), which is the main focus of this book, has unfolded under a context of greater political liberalization, with a livelier and freer press following the end of the Fujimori regime, and the opening of new outlets for political representation with the election of regional governments (chapter 3). Overall, figure 2 highlights the importance of political, rather than economic, conditions in providing a better explanation for the emergence of antimarket contention.

A few additional observations with relevance to the literature on the resurgence of antimarket contention can be drawn from the dataset. First, research that emphasizes the demobilizing effects of economic liberalization expects a widespread decline in mobilizations as market reforms move forward. For instance, Kurtz (2004) argues that market reforms destroy the organizational capacity of social resistance, especially through their effects on labor. Similarly, Oxhorn (2006) suggests that neoliberalism transforms citizenship into a relatively hollow kind of consumerism, ending distributional conflicts, or what Colburn (2002) characterizes as the "end of politics." Figure 3 compares the country's national level of strikes with protest for the period of my study. Paralleling trends in other Latin American countries, the graph reveals the changing basis of antigovernment mobilizations following Peru's transition to a market economy. This figure depicts the paradoxical effect of economic liberalization: it shows organized labor's decline in political clout, which made room for new actors and

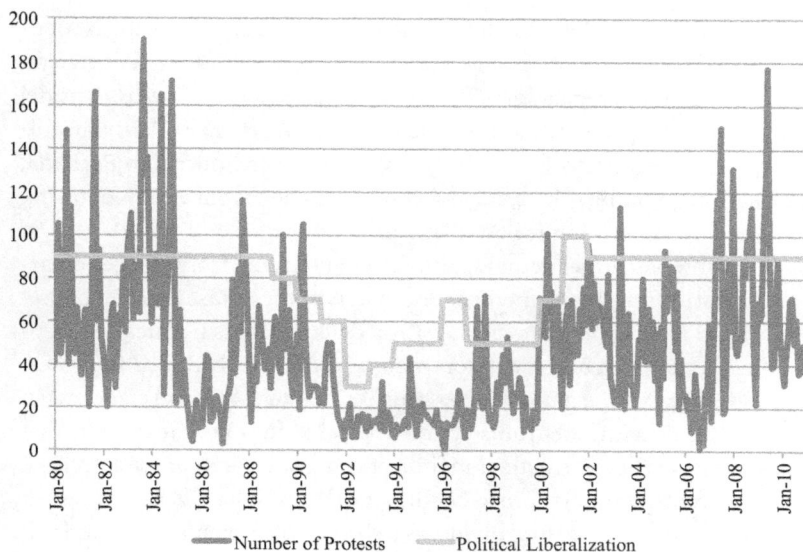

FIGURE 2. Contentious activity and political liberalization in Peru, 1980–2010. "Contentious activity" is the sum of all types of protest activity as recorded in the Base de Protestas Sociales del Perú (see the appendix). Political liberalization scores were taken from Freedom House. They represent the sum of the civil liberties and political rights indices, which range from 1 to 7, with lower values indicating greater freedom, yielding a theoretical range of 2 to 14 for the combined index. In the sample the combined Freedom House index ranges from 4 to 11. I reserved these values and added 14 to create a new scale from 30 to 100, with higher values indicating greater democracy. *Source:* Arce 2014.

other forms of popular resistance (see Arce 2008, 42). Put differently, whereas the traditional labor unions led popular mobilizations using strikes during the first wave of the early to mid-1980s, other sets of actors with a broader repertoire of protest would emerge during the second wave of mobilizations of the mid- to late 2000s (see figure 3).

The decline in labor activism can further be seen by comparing the number of workers who participate in strikes. On average, the number of workers involved in strikes was 508,840 during the 1980s, decreasing sharply to 81,107 during the 1990s, and even further to 3,813 during the 2000s.[14] The sharp decline in the level of strikes and workers participating in strikes suggests that vertical, national-level trade unions, such as the General Confederation of Peruvian Workers

(Confederación General de Trabajadores del Perú, CGTP), the National Federation of Miners, Metal and Steel Workers of Peru (Federación Nacional de Trabajadores Mineros, Metalúrgicos y Siderúrgicos del Perú, FNTMMSP), and the Sole Union of Workers of Peruvian Education (Sindicato Único de Trabajadores de la Educación Peruana, SUTEP), among others, no longer define national outcomes following the onset of economic liberalization.

However, other actors with greater autonomy from state and party institutions have emerged. For instance, the dataset shows that regional fronts (*frentes regionales*) and defense fronts (frentes de defensa) were the second most-common type of actor involved in protest events across the period 1980–2010. As chapters 4, 5, and 6 address in greater detail, these fronts are the typical kinds of organizations that emerge in the aftermath of mobilizations against extractive activities. The fronts exemplify broad coalitions of groups that cut across classes and the urban and rural divide, as well as environmental and national-

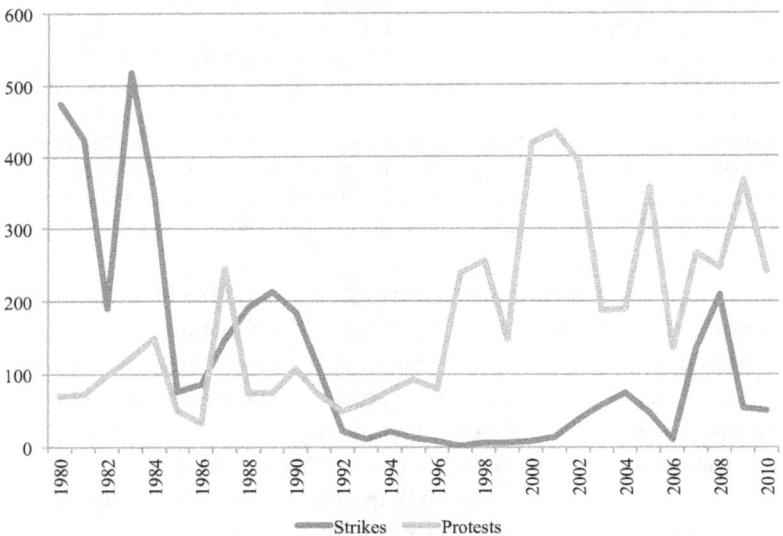

FIGURE 3. Strikes and protests in Peru, 1980–2010. Strikes and protests figures were taken from the Base de Protestas Sociales del Perú (see the appendix). Protests are the sum of mobilizations, roadblocks, sit-ins, and takeovers. *Source*: Arce 2014.

istic discourses. With few exceptions, most of these organizations did not gather up into national confederations or develop ties with political parties as part of a programmatic alternative to neoliberalism, yet their participation in protest events increased steadily during the first decade of the 2000s. Their repertoires of protest, including mobilizations, roadblocks, sit-ins, and takeovers, affected national outcomes and summarize well the repoliticization effects of economic liberalization (see chapter 1).

Second, research that dwells on the demobilizing effects of economic liberalization also suggests that exposure to worldwide competition produces a "powerless" postglobalization state with constrained capacities, particularly in the areas of monetary and fiscal policies, and as such, this literature has argued that the state no longer represents a worthy target of popular mobilization (Kurtz 2004, 271). In contrast, the dataset shows that the state remains the main target of contention, as 29.4 percent of mobilizations are directed at the ministries of the executive branch of government. After these ministries, the second most-common type of institution demanded is the central government (25.7 percent). As one would expect, the nature of the demands directed at the national government involved labor petitions. Altogether, this implies that popular subjects directed their demands to the state in an effort to seek some form of protection or compensation from market forces, even when economic liberalization policies succeeded in retiring the state from economic activities. These findings are consistent with Silva (2009, 28).

Using an original protest event dataset covering three decades of mobilizations, this chapter has evaluated two commonly held arguments regarding protest trends in Peru. These explanations include the state of the economy and the presence of political violence. As this chapter has shown, these arguments provide only partial clues to the long-term factors that have shaped mobilization and demobilization trends in the country. By widening the time horizon on the study of contentious activity in Peru, starting with the country's transition to democracy in 1980, and in congruence with political process theory's emphasis on political conditions from this book, this chapter has shown that the country's level of political liberalization was comparatively similar across the first wave of protest of the early to mid-1980s and the second wave in the mid- to late 2000s. Across these two periods, political democracy provided a favorable environment for collective protest. In the 1980s, the traditional labor unions were the main actor involved in mobilizations. In the 2000s, regional and defense fronts emerged as an important force in opposition to market policies, particularly in protests against extractive activities, and the state remained the main target of contention. Overall, the broader political context in which protests emerge provides a better explanation for different episodes of popular contention over the three decades under investigation.

Yet the conceptualization of democracy as an opportunity for mobilization cannot easily explain the variation of protest that exists within countries, particularly when the level of democracy remains time invariant. Why do apparently similar resource-abundant subnational units within the same national democratic regime have different levels of protest? Using the protest event dataset, and after illustrating the territorial unevenness of protest over time and space, the next chapter examines the effects of another formal dimension of political opportunities, as well as a central attribute of democracy—political competition—on subnational protests. As chapter 3 shows, the emphasis on political competition sheds light on how and why democracy matters at the subnational level. And the Peruvian case, in particular, provides an ideal setting to examine the effects of political competition amid weak institutions, given that the Peruvian party system of the 1980s came unglued with Fujimori's rise to power.

CHAPTER 3

MOBILIZATION BY EXTRACTION

Existing literature has shown that a country's abundance of natural resources is often associated with pervasive and negative outcomes, such as poor governance, low levels of economic development, civil war, and dictatorship (e.g., Karl 1997; Ross 1999; P. Collier and Hoeffler 2002, 2005; Dunning 2005; Fearon 2005; Humphreys 2005). These results have led some to speak of a "resource curse." With few exceptions, the bulk of this research has focused on cross-national comparisons, using aggregate national data that, more often than not, conceal significant within-nation heterogeneity and complexity. Moreover, the relationship between a country's geological endowments and contentious politics has rarely been systematically examined. Specifically, does the value of a country's geological wealth increase protests? If so, why, then, do apparently similar resource-abundant subnational units within the same national democratic regime have different levels of protest?

This chapter examines the relationship among resource wealth, political conditions, and protest across Peru's twenty-five regions. First, I outline the expansion of resource extraction following the economic liberalization policies of the 1990s and 2000s and its "structural" importance to the Peruvian economy as a whole and for subnational governments especially. Second, I present a framework to distinguish the different types of protest that are associated with resource wealth, explaining how resource extraction creates incentives for protest activity. Third, I revisit the political conditions that influence societal responses to resource extraction, specifically the underlying level of political competition across regional governments. As presented earlier, political competition captures another formal dimension of political opportunities as well as a central attribute of democracy. The fourth and final section of this chapter presents the results of the empirical analysis, showing how regional politics shapes subnational protest activity.

Mining in Peru

Large-scale mining in Peru developed in the central highlands of the country, involving the departments of Huancavelica, Junín, Pasco, and the northern provinces of the department of Lima. In the early 1900s, the operations of the Cerro de Pasco Corporation (CPC), an American mining company, expanded quickly, and CPC became "the only company in Peru to engage in the large-scale extraction, processing and commercialization of mineral ores and metals" (Kruijt and Vellinga 1979, 45). CPC bought concessions and smelters from competing mining companies in the area and a railroad line connecting all of its plants to one another and to the coast. The early history of large-scale extraction is also associated with the development of a labor movement of mining workers as CPC became the largest private employer in Peru. For example, the miner's confederation known as the National Federation of Miners, Metal and Steel Workers of Peru (FNTMMSP) traces its origins to the operations of CPC in the Central Andes (Kruijt and Vellinga 1979; Pajuelo 2010). The operations of CPC, however, ended with the reformist military regime of General Juan Velasco Alvarado (1968–75), which nationalized its holdings under the state-owned company known as Centromín Perú. The military also expropriated all of CPC's hacienda (estate), which covered a total of 247,000 hectares and included 87,284 sheep, 2,681 head of cattle, and 936 horses (Kruijt and Vellinga 1979, 54). Large haciendas like CPC's pushed peasants off their land, creating a surplus of laborers to work in the mines.

In the 1990s, the government of Alberto Fujimori (1990–2000) reversed this pattern of state ownership of so-called strategic industries and privatized Centromín Perú as well as hundreds of other state-owned enterprises (Arce 2005). Weakened by the economic crisis and political violence of the 1980s, the FNTMMSP resisted Fujimori's privatization goals, albeit unsuccessfully. In congruence with the intro-duction of market reforms, Fujimori made foreign investment in min-ing a very attractive industry. Mining claims by extractive companies skyrocketed from two million to fifteen million hectares during the 1990s and to twenty million in the late 2000s (see figure 4). Investment in mining rose from US $400 million in the 1980s and early 1990s to a record level of US $2.76 billion in 2009 (MEM 2004, 2010). Moreover, thirteen out of twenty-one member companies of the International Council on Mining and Metals (ICMM), the association of the world's largest mining companies, currently operate in Peru.[1] This is the high-est concentration of large mining companies in the Latin American region (Oxfam 2009). Thus, the increasing economic importance of resource extraction, specifically mining, rests on Fujimori's economic liberalization program.

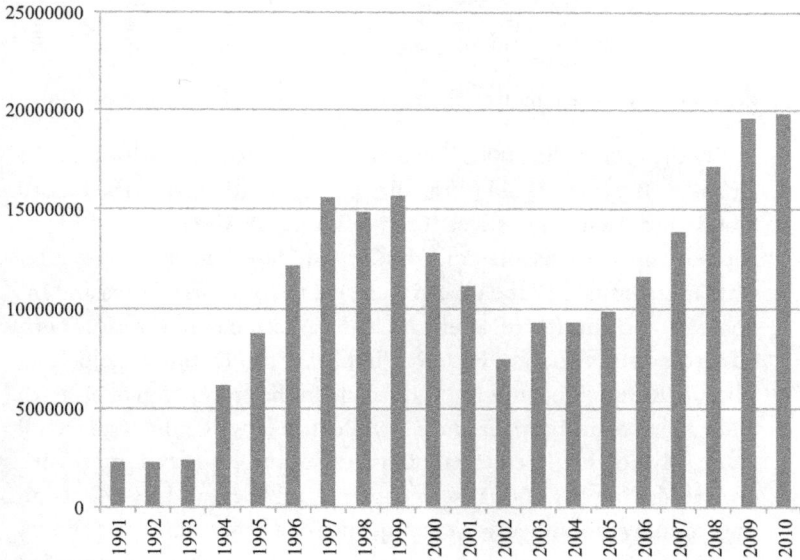

FIGURE 4. Mining concessions to private companies, 1991–2010 (in hectares). *Source*: CooperAción 2013.

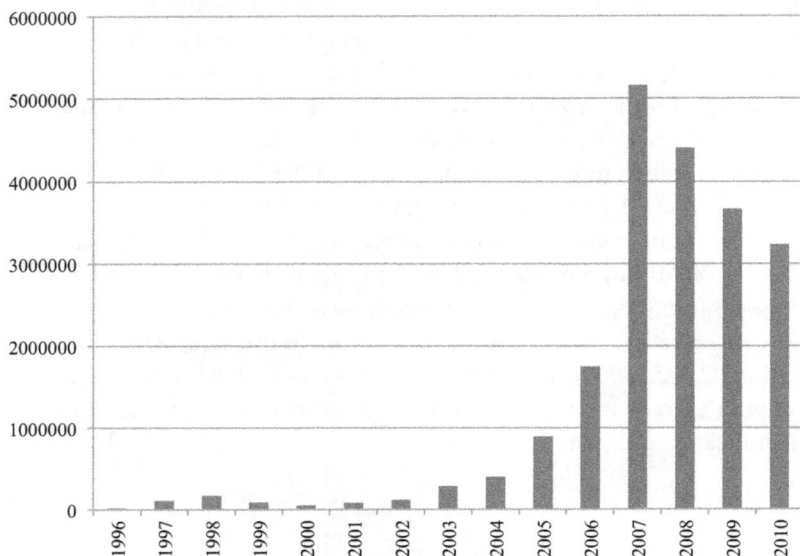

FIGURE 5. Mineral rents transferred to regions, 1996–2010. *Source*: INEI 2011.

By the end of the 2000s, Peru occupied a leading position in the global production of gold (fifth, after China, South Africa, the United States, and Australia), silver (first, followed by Mexico and China), copper (third, after Chile and the United States), lead (fourth, after China, Australia, and the United States), tin (third, after China and Indonesia), and zinc (third, after China and Australia). In the same period across Latin America, Peru was first in the production of gold, lead, silver, tellurium, tin, and zinc and second in the production of bismuth (after Mexico) and copper and molybdenum (after Chile) (Gurmendi 2008). Mining has been the main driver of the country's impressive growth during the 2000s (see chapter 2, table 2), and its effects on the economy multiplied as a consequence of a commodity price boom also during the same period. The price of gold, for instance, increased from US $344 in the early 1990s to US $1,225 in the late 2000s (per troy ounce). In the same period, the price of silver rose from US $4 to US $20 (per troy ounce), and the price of copper increased from US $1.03 to US $3.42 (per pound) (MEM 2010). In addition to rising commodity prices, the aggressive Chinese demand for raw materials has also contributed to this economic bonanza. In recent years, China has surpassed the United States as the main destination of Peru's exports. The exports include copper, iron, zinc, and fishmeal (BCRP 2012).

The central government accrued significant revenues from extractive industries, a portion of which is devolved to the regions where mining is located. The devolution of mineral rents changed considerably in the years leading up to, and immediately following, 2002, the year of the decentralization initiative (see chapter 2). Traditionally, 20 percent of the profit taxes paid by mining companies to the national government were transferred to subnational governments. However, during the late 1990s and early 2000s, the amount of mineral rents transferred to the regions had become more limited because these taxes, though legally prescribed, were not strictly enforced (Zavalla 2004, 169) (figure 5). Following the decentralization initiative, which called for the elections of regional governments to represent each of Peru's twenty-four departments and the constitutional province of Callao, new legislation was put in place to support the newly created subnational governments. Specifically, revenue transfers from profit taxes paid by mining companies increased to 50 percent. These transfers, as Avila, Viale, and Monge (2011, 164) explain, became "the main source of public investment for subnational governments." In short, the formation of regional governments created centrifugal forces for the rapid devolution of revenues to mining regions. The sequence of competitive regional elections (2002, 2006, and 2010) further expanded the political authority of regional presidents and, as a result, placed constraints on executive powers at the national level. Consequently, Lima's long-standing, centralized control of the regions began to erode.

Mining and Protest

Very few studies have examined the relationship between a country's geological wealth and contentious politics. As shown in chapter 2, Peru experienced a surge in protests by a variety of social actors after the fall of the Fujimori regime in 2000. Protests against the expansion of the extractive frontier are also the most common type of mobilizations taking place in the country (Arce 2008; Defensoría del Pueblo 2012).[2] Thus the resurgence of mobilizations overlaps considerably with the expansion of mining (figure 4), as well as rising mineral rents (figure 5). Here I advance a framework to differentiate the diversity of mobilizations surrounding resource extraction. I argue that some of these mobilizations are partly driven by "demands for rights," which are mostly in opposition to mining and seek to stop it; others are partly driven by "demands for services," which arise as a consequence of disputes over the distribution and use of revenues generated from resource extraction.[3]

Demands for Rights

Environmental concerns in defense of the water supply or the protection of agricultural lands exemplify the "demands for rights" category of mobilizations. The bulk of these mobilizations are in opposition to mining. In some cases, the environmental discourse seeks to prevent the initiation of mining activities, as in the case of Tambogrande in the province of Piura (chapter 4). In other cases, the environmental discourse seeks to halt the expansion of mining activities that are already present, as in Mount Quilish in the province of Cajamarca (chapter 5).

The perceived marginalization and exclusion of communities (in which resource extraction will take place) from the decision-making process regarding natural resource governance have also triggered a number of important protests. These mobilizations speak of consultation rights on development projects that affect indigenous people. The mobilization in opposition to the opening of the Amazon for development in Bagua (chapter 6) is an example of this category of protest involving "demand for rights," in this particular case, consultation and participation rights. Mobilizations invoking consultation rights often incorporate an environmentalist discourse as described above to further resist the exploitation of natural resources.

These mobilizations involve networks of actors in opposition to mining (e.g., local communities, local mayors, regional presidents, environmental NGOs, etc.) and networks of actors in support of extraction (e.g., the mining industry, the central government, business associations and chambers of commerce, the national media, etc.). Local communities and authorities where extractive activities occur are quick to denounce the perceived collusion between mining companies and the central government in awarding mining claims, as well as the lack of environmental oversight surrounding extractive activities. Aggrieved communities point out the overt conflict of interest of the

Ministry of Energy and Mines (MEM), which on the one hand awards mining rights to extractive companies and on the other hand assesses the environmental impact of mining projects on behalf of communities where mining takes place. As Bebbington et al. (2007) describe, the success of the MEM rests on its ability to expand mining; thus it is hardly unlikely that the ministry would seek to control anything. Generally, these environmental assessments are weak and focus mostly on initial exploration, not closure.

Demands for Services

Disputes over the distribution and use of revenues generated from natural resource extraction exemplify the "demands for services" category of mobilizations. These contentious episodes are not necessarily opposed to mining and often do not involve mining companies directly. Rather these mobilizations entangle local populations and political authorities representing the different tiers of government where the natural resource is extracted. These mobilizations are common in areas where mining may be the only activity that is economically viable and mining extraction is rarely in competition with other activities, such as agriculture. Regional governments thus seek to integrate extractive activities already present with the development of the local areas in which mining takes place.

In terms of the distribution of revenues, as shown in table 3, their allocation across different levels of government has changed over time. As several authors have suggested (Arellano-Yanguas 2010; Avila, Viale, and Monge 2011; Zavalla 2004), the perceived inequities in the distribution of revenues among presidents of regional governments, mayors of provincial municipalities, and mayors of district municipalities have triggered a sizeable number of protests.

In terms of the use of revenues, the disputes have to do with the efficient management of resource incomes, where efficient management refers to both its proper use and the capacity of subnational governments in delivering improvements where resource extraction takes place. These revenues are often spent in the delivery of services or infrastructure projects, such as roads, schools, and health centers.

A related set of mobilizations within this category of "demands for services" includes the renegotiations of previous land transfer agreements among mining companies, local communities, and authorities where the natural resource is extracted. Usually these renegotiations are triggered by sudden increases in mining profits. As Arellano-Yanguas (2010, 122) writes, rising mining profits encourage local communities to demand the "fulfilment of previous promises and agreements that they felt had not been honoured" or their fair share of company profits. Unlike the mobilizations over the distribution and use of revenues generated from resource extraction, these contentious episodes affect mining companies directly.

TABLE 3. Changes in the criteria for the distribution of mineral rents

Law 25506		Law 25007		Law 28332	
Approved 2001		Approved 2003		Approved 2004	
Beneficiary		Beneficiary		Beneficiary	
Regional government	20%	Regional government, plus 5 percent for public universities of the region	25%	Regional government, plus 5 percent for public universities of the region	25%
Municipalities of the province in which the resource is extracted	20%	Municipality of the district in which the resource is extracted	10%	Municipality of the district in which the resource is extracted	10%
		Municipalities of the province in which the resource is extracted, excluding the district of the mine	25%	Municipalities of the province in which the resource is extracted	25%
Municipalities of the region in which the resource is extracted	60%	Municipalities of the region in which the resource is extracted	40%	Municipalities of the region in which the resource is extracted	40%

Source: Arellano-Yanguas 2010, 20.

Note: Mineral rents do not include oil.

Mobilization by Extraction

A couple of additional points about this classification of mobilizations are warranted. First, the mobilizations involving "demands for rights" are less frequent but are often highly publicized, have national-level repercussions, and are arguably more important. These mobilizations, in fact, have shaped the decentralized allocation of revenues shown in table 3. To elaborate, the origins of mineral rents (*canon minero*)—which again represent the main source of public investment for the regional governments—mirror the creation of oil rents (*canon petrolero*). Oil rents were established in the mid-1970s. The beneficiaries of these intergovernmental transfers are the oil-producing departments of the Amazon region of Peru. The presence of mobilizations is a common denominator explaining the roots of both mineral and oil rents, suggesting the salience of social forces to understand the politics of decentralization, in particular fiscal policy. Arellano-Yanguas (2010, 112–13) adds that the mobilizations I have identified as "demands for rights" have influenced "the narratives, strategies and repertoires of contestation that people have subsequently employed elsewhere." The case studies in chapters 4, 5, and 6 of this book, therefore, deal with the category of mobilizations involving "demands for rights."[4]

Second, the differentiation between "demands for rights" and "demands for services" mirrors Perreault's (2006) discussion of demands for "procedural justice" and "distributive justice" over natural resource governance. Perreault (2006, 154) describes the demands for "procedural justice" as the ones calling for "greater participation and transparency in decisions over the management of natural resources." These demands overlap with what I have called "demands for rights" invoking prior consultation. In contrast, the demands for "distributive justice" represent those "calling for more equitable distribution of the benefits deriving from the exploitation of natural resources" (Perreault 2006, 154). These demands represent what I have called "demands for services" over the use and distribution of mineral wealth, including renegotiations of previous agreements between mining companies and local communities. When these demands are not met, Perreault (2006, 168) adds, resource extraction worsens "long-standing patterns of social inequality and political exclusion," especially among the rural poor. Unfulfilled demands, following the central ideas of this chapter, are also likely to foment protest activity.

The arguments of "greed" versus "grievance," commonly put forward by scholars of armed conflict on the causes of civil war (P. Collier and Hoeffler 2002, 2005), can also be extended to protest over natural resources. In this case, "demands for rights" approximate the grievances or economic threats that motivate people to engage in protest activity. In contrast, "demands for services" approach the notion of greed or economic opportunity insofar as individuals mobilize to better their situation, particularly in the presence of windfall profits as a consequence of rising commodity prices. More generally, grievances trace the "bad news" of extraction (i.e., damage to the environment or agriculture). Greed, in contrast, follows the "good news" of extraction (i.e., better provision of social services, higher wages for mine workers). From a perspective that emphasizes the importance of economic conditions, which is not the one favored in this book, both could also be seen as fomenting mobilizations, yet for different reasons.

Regional Politics

The election of regional presidents that began with the process of decentralization in 2002 sought to advance the supposed virtues of decentralization, which are often advocated by the international donor community, democratic theorists, and local activists. According to its proponents, local officials, such as regional presidents, by virtue of their close association with local conditions, are more likely to take into account the concerns of local communities, which in the past were freely ignored by the central government. In turn, citizens are more likely to participate in local politics, where they can more easily influence outcomes and thus hold regional presidents accountable by virtue of their proximity. Thus, the anticipated outcome of the decentralization process is greater accountability and responsiveness that will then lead to better local governments.[5] Following this logic, the election of regional presidents was meant to improve resource governance. However, as discussed below, the new outlets for political representation advanced by the decentralization process have been flooded by amateur politicians and weak parties that have little or no connection to, or support from, national parties. The presence of weakly developed parties thus impaired the mechanisms of accountability and responsiveness that are typically associated with electoral competition (chapter 1) and encouraged the use of confrontational, disruptive strategies to achieve political goals or express policy demands. In some cases, regional governments became an easy target for protest. In other cases, they actively encouraged mobilizations in opposition to extraction. In both cases, they complicated resource governance.

The parties contesting regional elections do not provide adequate points of access to shape policy, irrespective of their number or proximity to voters as a consequence of decentralization. These parties are very personalistic and ephemeral (Levitsky 2013). Very few regional parties prevail beyond a single election or two, and on average almost two-thirds of the parties in each regional elections are new parties (Seifert 2011). Moreover, across the three regional elections of 2002, 2006, and 2010, regional parties have won office with an average of 30 percent of the regional vote. Similarly, the average effective number of parties (ENP) competing in these three regional elections was 5.25, with a minimum of 1.7 parties in the northern region of Lambayeque in 2010 and a maximum of 8.86 parties in the southern region of Puno, also in 2010 (see table 4). The level of political fragmentation across the regions (5.25 parties) is greater than that of the national legislature, which approximates 4 parties across the 2001, 2006, and 2011 national elections.[6] In response to the fragile bases of support for regional governments, starting with the regional elections of 2010, the central government stipulated a plurality of 30 percent to win office, which would then offset a runoff election between the top two contenders. In the 2010 regional election cycle, there were ten runoff elections nationwide, representing 40 percent of all the regions.

Several authors have also observed the dealignment between parties representing the national government (located in the coastal capital of Lima) and parties representing regional governments (Vergara 2011). This disassociation reflects the fluidity and weakness of the Peruvian party system (see chapter 2). While in office, for instance, Toledo's Perú Posible controlled only one regional government (Callao), and García's APRA controlled two regional governments (La Libertad and Piura).[7] Across the three regional elections of 2002, 2006, and 2010, APRA is the only national-level party that has had an important presence across regional governments, but the party's gains were not long lasting. During the first regional elections of 2002, APRA won twelve regions (or 48 percent of all regions). Yet APRA only controlled two regions after the 2006 elections and only one region after the 2010 elections. The bulk of regional governments are controlled by a large number of independent candidates who are only loosely connected to any party organization at all.

TABLE 4. Average results for regional elections, 2002, 2006, and 2010

Election	Winner's Share	Min.	Max.	ENP	Min.	Max.	N
2002	28.10	19.28	50.90	5.63	3.06	8.12	25
2006	31.49	18.80	49.61	5.27	2.73	8.21	25
2010	31.80	18.52	49.75	5.43	2.84	8.86	25
2010 runoff	43.20	18.52	71.08	3.69	1.70	7.71	10

Source: ONPE 2012.

Note: "Min." (minimum) and "Max." (maximum) are the lowest and highest share of votes, respectively, for the winner of the regional presidency. "Min." (minimum) and "Max." (maximum) are the lowest and highest values of ENP, respectively.

The fragmented multiparty environment found in the Peruvian regional elections (ENP is greater than 5), and considering the ability of regional movements to win a subnational presidency with very low percentages of the vote (18 percent in several cases), suggests that these regional parties do not need to mobilize support across all groups of society or make broad appeals to their constituents. These parties instead "have an incentive to focus their attention on smaller segments of the voting population" (Chhibber and Nooruddin 2004, 171). Moreover, rather than providing public goods, these parties are more likely to distribute club or private goods to the groups they are courting (Chhibber and Nooruddin 2004). Along these lines, Levitsky (2013, 303) argues that the fluidity of regional parties allows politicians to pursue their "naked ambitions" rather than some longer-term public good. Because these politicians quickly jump from one party to the next, their ambitions simply go unchecked by the party organizations that sponsor them.[8] These ideas are other ways to explain how the presence of weak parties at the subnational level in Peru thwarts the responsive effects that are often attributed to political competition. For this reason, in the empirical analysis I speak about political fragmentation rather than political competition as described in previous chapters.

To summarize, the presence of weak parties across several regional elections (2002, 2006, and 2010) damaged the mechanisms of accountability and responsiveness that are often associated with electoral competition (see chapter 1). In other words, regional elections, rather than enhancing the connection between public preferences and government output, strained this connection. As a result, protest activity became the preferred mechanism to influence those who govern, and even more so in a context of rising mineral rents (figure 5).

A Subnational Comparative Analysis

In examining the relationship among resource wealth, regional politics, and protest across Peru's twenty-five regions, the subnational comparative analysis presented in this chapter corrects for the national bias of the existing literature when studying the rise of popular contention after Latin America's third democratic wave. It allows us to coalesce changing patterns of mobilization and demobilization within a single country, all of which helps us to formulate better causal inferences on the factors that shape protest activity locally and over time. Therefore, the unit of analysis is the region-year.

The dependent variable PROTEST is the annual number of protests taken from the Base de Protestas Sociales del Perú and is based on the print media (Arce 2014) (for a description of the dataset, see the appendix). These data measure the variation of protest activity across Peru's twenty-five regions and across time in each region (for descriptive statistics, see chapter 2, table 2).[9] To be clear, the dependent variable does not restrict protest to solely contentious episodes involving resource extraction, as in Arellano-Yanguas (2010). Restricting protest to contentious episodes involving resource extraction provides little variation on the main dependent variable of interest: virtually all episodes of protest involving resource extraction include some level of mineral revenues.

My main explanatory variables of interest are MINERAL RENT and POLITICAL FRAGMENTATION. First, MINERAL RENT is the annual canon minero transfers per capita at current values. The canon minero represents the devolution of mineral revenues collected by the central government to subnational governments (Zavalla 2004). This variable directly measures the value of a region's geological endowment, which is determined by the quantity and quality of minerals that are available, as well as the investment made in extracting these minerals at any given time. In the sample, the measure ranges from a high of 1,277 Peruvian soles for the region of Moquegua to a low of less than 1 Peruvian sol for the region of Lambayeque. If the extraction of natural resources is harmful due to unfulfilled "demands for rights" or "demands for services," MINERAL RENT should be positively correlated with protest. In short, this variable serves a useful indicator of resource-based grievances.

Second, POLITICAL FRAGMENTATION is the effective number of political parties competing in the regional elections of 2002, 2006, and 2010 using Laakso and Taagepera's (1979) formula. Because not all regional parties are created equal, the measure weights each regional party by the number of votes it receives, preventing the count from being inflated by very small regional parties (for descriptive statistics, see table 4). POLITICAL FRAGMENTATION implies the presence of a large number of independent regional movements that are elected with fragile pluralities. I theorize that higher levels of POLITICAL FRAGMENTATION impair the mechanisms of accountability and responsiveness that are typically associated with electoral competition (see chapter 2). Therefore, POLITICAL FRAGMENTATION should be positively correlated with protest.[10]

My control variables are GDP MINING, POVERTY, and POPULATION (LOG). GDP MINING is the share of mining production in relation to the total GDP of the region at constant 1994 prices. This variable is used as a proxy for the level of mining activity in a given area. The variable POVERTY is the percentage of the regional population below the poverty line in terms of income measured against a region-specific variable demarcation of poverty. It is used as a proxy for the economic grievances that are said to increase protest activity. The variable POPULATION (LOG) seeks to control for the possibility that more populated regions would experience higher levels of mobilization compared to less populated regions. All of the variables in the analysis are measured annually for each region. To control for the temporal dependence of protest activity, I include the lagged dependent variable PROTEST$_{t-1}$. Tarrow (1998), among others, argues that protests follow a cyclical pattern in which waves of protest increase rapidly in some periods and then recede in the same manner in other periods.

I proceed by estimating an unconditional, fixed-effects negative binomial event-count model. Event-count models use maximum likelihood estimation to assess the probability of event occurrences. As event counts always take on nonnegative integer values, the distribution of events is skewed and discrete, producing errors that are not normally distributed or homoskedastic (Long 1997). In addition, overdispersion and goodness-of-fit tests indicated that a negative binomial model is the best method of estimation for my data. I estimate an unconditional fixed-effects version of the negative binomial model in order to account for unobserved (or unobservable) unit heterogeneity in the data. Simply put, I need to control for all of the idiosyncratic factors that may make a particular region more or less protest prone. I accomplish this by including a set of regional dummy variables in the regression model—one for each region in the sample, minus one. Because I am concerned about the nonindependence of observations within regions over time, I present the models below with robust standard errors clustered by region.

Empirical Results

The analysis is divided into two sections. The first part examines the relationship between resource wealth and protest using the earliest data available involving mineral rents, which is 1996. As noted earlier, resource extraction by large mining companies resumes with the economic liberalization policies of the 1990s under Fujimori. The second part of the analysis builds on these results and examines the effects of regional politics on protest by taking into account the underlying level of political fragmentation across the regional elections of 2002, 2006, and 2010.

Table 5 presents the results of the first part of the analysis. To better capture the effects of resource wealth on protests locally and over time, table 5 splits the data before (model 1) and after the decentralization process of 2002 (models 2 and 3). As reported in model 1, the variable MINERAL RENT has no effect on protest prior to Toledo's decentralization. In contrast, in model 2 the variable MINERAL RENT has a positive and statistically significant effect on the level of subnational protest. The results in model 2 were also robust to the exclusion of regional dummy variables (see model 3). The models in table 5 present trimmed results, controlling only for the log of population and the lagged dependent variable PROTEST$_{t-1}$. These trimmed results help to confirm that the effects of resource wealth on protest are not driven by the inclusion of control variables.

The comparison of the results before and after Toledo's decentralization initiative suggests that something changed with the arrival of regional governments starting in 2002. For the period 1996–2001, in fact, resource wealth is not statistically correlated with protest. At that time, resource wealth was centrally controlled, and the absence of political organizations at the subnational level (e.g., regional governments) did not provide an outlet to articulate possible "demands for rights" or "demands for services" over the extraction of natural resources. For the period 2002–10, in contrast, the statistical results suggest that resource wealth increased the incidence of protest. Arellano-Yanguas (2010, 89) summarizes this association as "more money, more conflicts," though his analysis only focused on the 2005–8 period, when mineral commodity prices were already on the rise. Paradoxically, as the next set of results discusses (table 6), the introduction of regional government did not serve to improve resource governance.

TABLE 5. Mineral rent and protest before and after decentralization

	Model 1 (1996–2001)	Model 2 (2002–10)	Model 3 (2002–10)
Mineral rent	0.0009 (0.0031)	0.0002*** (0.0001)	0.0004*** (0.0001)
Population (log)	23.51*** (2.582)	2.094* (1.112)	0.624*** (0.0810)
Protest$_{t-1}$	−0.0068*** (0.0026)	0.0007 (0.0010)	0.0049*** (0.0011)
Region dummies	Yes	Yes	No
Constant	−299.4*** (32.98)	−24.38* (14.28)	−5.747*** (1.050)
Observations	139	217	217
Log likelihood	−382.8	−785.5	−812.3
α	0.213	0.283	0.389

Notes: Robust standard errors are in parentheses; *** p<0.01, ** p<0.05, * p<0.1. All models are unconditional fixed effects negative binomial regressions.

Table 6 incorporates the effects of regional politics by examining the underlying level of political fragmentation across the three regional elections of 2002, 2006, and 2010. As shown in this table, the variable POLITICAL FRAGMENTATION correlates positively with the level of subnational protest in a statistically significant fashion. The results in the trimmed model 5 were robust to the exclusion of regional dummy variables (see model 4). The effects of POLITICAL FRAGMENTATION also remain positive and statistically significant with the inclusion of the variable MINERAL RENT (model 6), as well as the control variables POVERTY and GDP MINING (model 7).

As previously discussed, the decentralization process advanced new outlets for political representation at the subnational level, and these new outlets, by virtue of their proximity to local conditions, should in principle boost the connection between public preferences and government output. These new outlets could also be seen as points of access to shape policy, inviting assimilative strategies for groups to work through the established political institutions. However, amateur politicians, elected with fragile pluralities and few ties to national-level parties, make up the bulk of regional governments. The parties at the regional level are also better described as personalistic vehicles that rarely endure from one election to the next. Consequently, the presence of weak parties at the regional level impaired the electoral connection between competition, on the one hand, and accountability and responsiveness, on the other, and encouraged the use of protest activity to achieve political goals or express policy demands. All said, while the empirical results suggest that resource wealth and regional politics affect the level of subnational protest, the effect of resource wealth is visible only after the decentralization initiative took place. For this reason, I have argued that the relationship between protest and subnational political conditions is closer than that between protest and natural resource rents, which again can be seen as a useful indicator of resource-based grievances. It is also worth reiterating that the political environment in the post-Fujimori period was simply more favorable to mobilization (see chapter 2).

To give more substantive interpretations around the quantities of interest, I now provide the effect of MINERAL RENT and POLITICAL FRAGMENTATION using a statistical simulation. Based on King, Tomz, and Wittenberg (2000), table 7 presents the predicted event counts of PROTEST with statistical uncertainty using model 7 (table 6). The predicted event counts of PROTEST are computed for three different levels of MINERAL RENT and POLITICAL FRAGMENTATION (low, mean, and high), based on their minimum, mean, and maximum values in the sample. All the estimates are statistically significant at the conventional level. First, the predicted number for PROTEST almost triples, from 16.20 at the low level of MINERAL RENT to 46.65 at the high level of MINERAL RENT. Second, the predicted number for PROTEST almost doubles, from 12.96 at the low level of POLITICAL FRAGMENTATION to 22.48 at the high level of POLITICAL FRAGMENTATION.

TABLE 6. Political fragmentation, mineral rent, and protest, 2002–10

	Model 4	Model 5	Model 6	Model 7
Political fragmentation	0.0658** (0.0298)	0.0900** (0.0390)	0.0893** (0.0373)	0.0981** (0.0390)
Mineral rent			0.0002*** (0.0001)	0.0002*** (0.001)
Poverty				−0.0001 (0.0076)
GDP mining				1.210 (1.466)
Population (log)	0.547*** (0.0809)	3.587*** (1.001)	2.932** (1.140)	3.107 (1.999)
Protest$_{t-1}$	0.0055*** (0.0012)	0.0016 (0.0010)	0.0014 (0.0010)	0.0015 (0.0010)
Region dummies	No	Yes	Yes	Yes
Constant	−4.984*** (1.060)	−44.04*** (12.93)	−35.62** (14.73)	−37.91 (26.08)
Observations	225	225	217	210
Log likelihood	−845.1	−811.0	−783.2	−760.0
α	0.407	0.277	0.275	0.269

Notes: Robust standard errors are in parentheses; *** $p<0.01$, ** $p<0.05$, * $p<0.1$. All models are unconditional fixed effects negative binomial regressions.

TABLE 7. Estimated effects of political fragmentation and mineral rents on protest

	Minimum	Mean	Maximum
Political fragmentation	12.96 (1.80)	17.51 (0.89)	22.48 (2.05)
Mineral rent	16.20 (0.83)	17.51 (0.89)	46.65 (13.69)

Note: Entries are the estimated event counts of PROTEST, calculated using Clarify 2.1. The levels of political fragmentation and mineral rents are measured around minimum, mean, and maximum values in the sample. The minimum values indicate low levels; the maximum values indicate high levels. Standard errors are in the parentheses.

This empirical analysis also helps to explain why apparently similar resource-abundant regions within Peru experience different levels of protest. To elaborate, Tacna, Ancash, Cusco, and Pasco are resource-rich regions, and their government coffers are overflowing with mineral rents. Including the region of Moquegua, and similar to Arellano-Yanguas (2010, 16), these are the top five regions receiving the greatest volume of mineral rents.[11] In the sample, for instance, the region of Tacna is the second-largest recipient of mineral rents in the country (1,011 soles per capita), followed by the region of Ancash (547 soles per capita), the region of Cusco (493 soles per capita), and the region of Pasco (438 soles per capita). However, the level of political fragmentation in Ancash (5.9 parties) and Cusco (5.9 parties) is higher than the sample mean (5.25 parties) and also higher compared to the regions of Tacna (4.8 parties) and Pasco (4.9 parties). Accordingly, the regions of Ancash (25.7 protests) and Cusco (42.7 protests) have more protests than the sample mean of 17.6 (excluding the region of the capital city of Lima) and the regions of Tacna (14.7 protests) and Pasco (8.7 protests).

In this chapter, I have argued that the association between resource extraction and protest is likely due to unfulfilled "demands for rights" or "demands for services." But a grievance-centered approach that solely emphasizes unfulfilled demands or injustices, regardless of their type, does not provide a complete account of the incidence of subnational protest activity. Following the central argument of this book, this chapter brings political conditions back into the analysis of antimarket contention. At the subnational level, it focuses on the salience of political competition, which is seen as both another dimension of political opportunities and a central attribute of democracy. Yet because regional politics have grown increasingly fragmented and fluid, in the empirical analysis I speak about political fragmentation rather than competition. And the empirical results show that regional politics affect protest activity, but in a manner opposite to what advocates of decentralization had anticipated. The presence of weak regional parties, rather than improving decisions over resource governance, led to the escalation of protest activity as a mechanism to influence those who govern.

Commenting on the 2011 presidential elections, Harvard political science professor Steven Levitsky noted that President García "governed with laziness."[12] His comments had to do with the inconsistency of an economic boom and government inaction. Although the economy experienced high levels of economic growth, approximating 6 percent of GDP in the decade of the 2000s, the García administration did not address the growing disparities and social exclusion that had reinforced the long-standing cleavage between the coast and the highlands of Peru. García, like Toledo before him, focused on sustaining economic growth and attracting foreign investment. But achieving these goals required bolstering the confidence of investors, and widespread protests counteracted efforts to improve the country's investment climate.

Both governments were generally passive in response to the hundreds of protests that surfaced around the country. Their passivity came about from the expectation that "growth from commodities would trickle down over time" (Cameron 2011b, 46). It also reflected their anticipation that the newly created regional governments would step up to resolve these protests. However, as this chapter has shown, the political fragility of regional authorities actively encouraged mobilizations against mining and the central government's support for these activities. These mobilizations became "everyday forms of [collective] resistance" (Scott 1986) and thus complicated the government's efforts to expand the extractive frontier. As subsequent chapters discuss in further detail, Toledo and García did not have a clear strategy to deal with rising protests. It appeared that their governments strung protestors along, expecting perhaps that these mobilizations would die down as a consequence of protest fatigue.

Having shed light on the factors that explain the variation of subnational protest within Peru, the second half of the book shifts attention to the consequences of mobilizations. The case studies presented in chapters 4, 5, and 6 show how strategic framing allowed opposition groups to build associational power (i.e., organizational capacity) and collective power (i.e., coalitional capacity). In addition, in several of the mobilizations against the extraction of natural resources, agriculture-based organizations as well as NGOs were instrumental for the emergence of successful collective action and, as such, reflect the salience of resource mobilization as a critical ingredient in a protest movement's ability to organize. To summarize, insofar as political conditions were favorable, both framing processes and resource mobilization transformed localized, segmented outbursts against resource extraction into larger opposition movements that affected national-level politics. While these mobilizations did not "scale up" to topple promarket presidents, as had taken place in other Latin American countries, they altered the course of elected officials' governing agenda.[13]

PART II
COMPARATIVE CASES

CHAPTER 4

LIME WARS

In 1949, the World Bank and the Peruvian government undertook massive investments aimed at the agricultural development of the Tambogrande region. Located on the western coast of Peru in the northern department of Piura, this geographic area was originally known for its arid lands and lack of economic productivity. However, after successfully diverting water from the Quiroz River into the local basin, the irrigation project transformed the Tambogrande region into a very productive agricultural valley. The project underwent numerous stages, with various levels of international and domestic investment, and its benefits are still clear over half a century later. The region produces a diverse breed of crops including limes, mangos, rice, cotton, and corn. Limes and mangos, in particular, are permanent crops, representing approximately two-thirds of the agricultural production from the area, and account for approximately half of the national yield (Lowrie 2002). Almost two-thirds of the local population draw their living from agriculture, and agricultural crops provide a significant source of income to local farmers.[1]

The Tambogrande area, however, is also very rich in minerals like gold and copper. The business sector's interest in exploiting these resources dates back to the early 1980s, yet the mining project, then led by a French company, never got off the ground. The most recent antimining mobilization in Tambogrande, which began in 1999 and ended in 2003, surged as a consequence of renewed business efforts in extracting the region's minerals. This latest effort involved a Canadian company called Manhattan Minerals Corporation (MMC). As in the early 1980s, the most recent antimining protest pitted agrarian elites, supported by local and regional politicians, against foreign and domestic mining interests. However, in contrast to the political scenario of the 1980s, the governments of Alberto Fujimori and Alejandro Toledo emerged as key allies in support of large-scale mining, given that both governments came to view resource extraction as a source of economic growth. In the end, agricultural interests prevailed and successfully stalled mining extraction in the region.

The success of agrarian elites hinged on their organizational strength, as well as an effective framing campaign in opposition to mining. Consistent with the typology of protest outcomes outlined in table 1 (chapter 1), mining and agriculture were in competition with each other in Tambogrande. And the agricultural economy of the area made available a number of preexisting organizations, such as producers' associations (asociaciones de productores) and water users' boards (junta de usuarios de riego), which gradually coalesced into a larger organization in opposition to extraction. This organization was known as the San Lorenzo Valley and Tambogrande Defense Front (Frente de Defensa del Valle de San Lorenzo y Tambogrande, FDVST). The front drew upon the support of other organizations outside Tambogrande, creating an even larger coalition in opposition to mining. The front's strategic framing campaign, which connected the production of limes with the nation's cultural identity, was instrumental for aggrieved groups to build both associational power and collective power and produced high levels of collective action compared to other cases. The mobilization in Tambogrande was also the first to invoke a popular referendum in opposition to extraction, a political strategy that has been replicated in other protests against mining and with the same political objective.

I begin this chapter by describing the three key episodes of contention that unfolded during the "battle" for Tambogrande: the February 2001 strikes, the June 2002 referendum in opposition to mining, and the 2003 resistance campaign known as the "lime war" (*la guerra del limón*). The next section of this chapter examines the organizational strength of aggrieved groups and the mining industry's response to the opposition forces. The chapter concludes by analyzing the effects of these events on local and national politics.

From Protest to Referendum

The start of mining concessions in Tambogrande dates back a few decades. In 1979, the Ministry of Energy and Mines (MEM) extended mining rights to the French state-owned company Bureau de Recherches Géologiques et Minières (BRGM). The project, however, never got off the ground due to the absence of a legal framework conducive to the exploration and exploitation of the site (De Echave et al. 2009, 23). Several years later, in 1990, the Peruvian legislature changed course and sanctioned a national law deeming the Tambogrande project of "national necessity." Law 25284 also provided a path for BRGM to sell its rights to a more able company, while also granting the state-owned company Centromín Perú 25 percent of the shares in the project. In 1996, BRGM sold their rights to the Canadian company Manhattan Minerals Corporation (MMC).

In late 1999, MMC declared it had plans to begin construction on an open-pit mine for the extraction of gold. Because of the size of the project, the plan called for the relocation of eight thousand residents, out of a town of only sixteen thousand inhabitants.[2] MMC also announced that many of the local tributaries of the Piura River, which runs through the town, had to be diverted in order to meet their large water needs. This diversion threatened the agricultural economy that had developed in the region. The relocation of about half of the town's residents and the danger that mining posed to the agriculture-based economy epitomize well the two core issues that motivated aggrieved opposition groups to resist mining. These core issues led to a sustained mobilization, with the scale and intensity of contention developing over three key episodes of popular resistance: the February 2001 strikes, the June 2002 referendum in opposition to mining activities, and the 2003 resistance campaign known as the "lime war" (la guerra del limón). All of these events unfolded over a more favorable environment for mobilization, following the end of the Fujimori regime. As shown below, over time the strategies of the opposition changed greatly, from confrontational to assimilative, moving away from violence and embracing consultative mechanisms against extraction. In order to mount a sustained mobilization, residents of Tambogrande had to build associational and collective power that could rival the resources of MMC, as well as construct a frame that could entice support from other groups beyond the local population of farmers who were strongly against mining.

The San Lorenzo Valley and Tambogrande Defense Front (FDVST) emerged as the leading antimining coalition against MMC. Led by Francisco ("Pancho") Ojeda Riofrío, and with the support of farmers organized in several producer organizations, the FDVST was quick in its response to reject the mine and initially worked to organize local demonstrations, which were mostly restricted to strike activity but sometimes escalated to roadblocks.[3] With the mine's entrance points blocked, MMC's workers were unable to gain access to the exploration site, limiting progress. These sorts of provocations occurred more frequently in the early stages of the campaign and escalated with each new demonstration. It was a commonly held belief early in the campaign that by slowing the exploration phase of the future mine, the FDVST could persuade MMC to abandon the project entirely.

In February 2001, the defense front organized a general strike in Tambogrande, hoping to demonstrate the district's solidarity against the project; this general strike became one of the high points of contention (Muradian, Martinez-Alier, and Correa 2003, 780; Olortegui 2007, 33). On February 27 and 28, the strike turned into protests through the main streets of Tambogrande and in front of MMC's camp in the town. The protest became violent when a number of demonstrators stormed the offices of MMC, burning machinery and the model homes that had been built for the relocation of Tambogrande residents. Hundreds of police officers sought to protect the property of MMC, and during the clash with the police, fifteen residents and twenty-five police officers were wounded, and several residents were arrested. Following the incident, MMC moved its operations to the nearby city of Piura and filed a lawsuit against the leaders of the defense front. The lawsuit charged the group with "intellectual responsibility" for the physical damages made to their property, which approached over half a million dollars (De Echave et al. 2009, 35). One account described the event as follows: "On February 2001, we organized a strike asking the mining company to leave Tambogrande. Since the 26th at 11:30 p.m. the police attacked us launching tear gases. . . . There were more than 600 police officers and 15,000 Tambograndinos, in front of

Manhattan's camp. It was an unmanageable situation. . . . The population broke the police's shields in pieces, and we had to rescue some police officers otherwise they would have been murdered" (quoted in Olortegui 2007, 33).

Following the events of the February strikes came even more violence with the assassination of Godofredo García Baca a month later.[4] García Baca was the president of the Association of Mango Producers and a local leader who opposed mining in the area during the 1980s and did so again in the late 1990s and early 2000s, with the arrival of MMC. The assassination of García Baca had a profound effect on changing the tone and methods of further disputes. Leaders of the FDVST began to watch more closely the activities of the organizations that supported the front and emphasized the need to moderate the tone of the campaign. The leaders now believed the best way of communicating their opposition was through a direct referendum by the people. Although always on the table, the suggestion of using the consultation mechanism following a long period of hostility established a change in the character of the small town, and its effect would be profound in Tambogrande and elsewhere in the coming years.

In June 2002, the defense front, with the support of the mayor of Tambogrande, Alfredo Rengifo Navarrete, organized the referendum vote in the district of Tambogrande.[5] Over 73 percent of thirty-six thousand eligible voters participated in the referendum, and 98 percent of voters rejected the mining project (De Echave et al. 2009, 38). The referendum's outcome was clear: the people did not want mining in their district.

Showing support for MMC, and arguing that the referendum lacked legal substance because it had not been undertaken through the proper electoral channels, the central government went ahead with the mining project's environmental assessment process. Specifically, the MEM put forth a procedure for the submission of an environmental impact report (estudio de impacto ambiental, EIA) to be completed. The presentation of the EIA allowed for informative meetings with the local population, including public hearings in which grievances could be addressed in a civil manner. This presentation of the EIA was also a way for the government to show that it was not totally overlooking the demands of aggrieved groups.[6]

The Lime War

Starting in early 2003 and continuing through the year, the FDVST coordinated a series of demonstrations that became known as the "lime war." These demonstrations heightened the importance of the production of limes to traditional Peruvian dishes, as slogans from protestors sought to "save the ceviche" ("salvemos el ceviche") (ceviche is a traditional national dish of fish marinated in lime sauce) (Paredes 2008, 296). The front's strategic framing was successful in connecting the local, lime-based economy with the nation's cultural identity. With these demonstrations, protestors also demanded recognition of the results of the June 2002 popular referendum, which the National Society of Mining, Petroleum, and Energy (Sociedad Nacional de Minería, Petróleo y Energía, SNMPE), the leading mining business organization based in Lima, declared to be illegal. The demonstrations were set up to coincide with the days that the public hearings for the presentation of the EIA were to be held. Protestors sought to dissuade the public from participating in the EIA talks, believing they were only a show to mask the true intentions of MMC: to continue with the extractive process unabated. Three hearings were scheduled to be held in November 2003: one in Tambogrande, one in Lima, and one in Piura. These three hearings, however, were suspended due to the mobilizations led by the defense front and its supporting organizations based in Lima and Piura.

Surprisingly, on December 12, 2003, the state-owned company Centromín Perú, MMC's partner, announced that MMC did not meet the established financial and logistical requirements that were stipulated in the original concession contract. Among other things, MMC would have to prove a net patrimony of US $100 million and further show evidence that the company was able to treat ten thousand tons of minerals per day. With this announcement, which was made by the minister of MEM, Hans Fleury, the government rescinded approval of the project, and the Tambogrande concession was terminated.

To summarize, the opposition campaign led by the defense front initially orchestrated confrontational, disruptive strategies that produced both material losses and human casualties. Following the death of García Baca, however, the leaders of the FDVST became more restrained in their actions, turning to assimilative strategies and participatory mechanisms in opposition to MMC. They invoked a referendum with the support of the local mayor and began enlisting the support of other organizations beyond the town of Tambogrande. These changes reflected the growing associational and collective power of the defense front, as well as its successful framing in opposition to mining.

Tambogrande's Associational and Collective Power

Agrarian elites portrayed the region of Tambogrande and San Lorenzo as a successful agricultural frontier with the right of self-determination against mining corporations. The success of agrarian elites in stopping MMC hinged on their ability to build associational power (i.e., their organizational capacity to create new organizations or recast existing ones) and collective power (i.e., their coalitional capacity to forge alliances across new or recast organizations).[7] As explained below, these organizations influenced the regional and national perceptions of the impracticality of resource extraction and included local, national, and international support networks. Each level emphasized a different frame, and these frames ranged from economic survival to national identity to democratic ideals.

At the local level, the grassroots organization known as the defense front, consisting mostly of farmers and peasants, opposed the development of the mine. The defense front was created in August 1999, and in the beginning it had a collegial presidency consisting of three individuals: Napoleón Nathals Juárez, Eduardo Monteza Alama, and Francisco Ojeda Riofrío. Over time, however, Ojeda Riofrío assumed leadership of the front. He was subsequently elected mayor of Tambogrande for the period 2003–6, and the start of his mayoral term overlapped with the culmination of the antimining protest. As discussed earlier, the defense front was involved in the three key episodes of contention that unfolded during the "battle" for Tambogrande.

The front was successful in articulating the view that mining was a threat to the agricultural way of life of Tambogrande and not necessarily compatible with agriculture, as MMC had argued. It presented several arguments to demonstrate that farming represented the only form of economic subsistence for much of the population. For instance, the life of the mine would be approximately seventeen years, and the gains in employment from mining would not be sufficient to compensate for the loss of jobs in farming, which date back to the late 1940s. Supporters of the front argued that MMC provided biased reports concerning the benefits of mining because all of the information was "colored positively" ("todo era siempre positivo") (Paredes 2008, 277).

At the national level, the defense front developed a large network of support working with Lima- and other Piura-based NGOs. These NGOs worked in diverse areas, such as human rights, conflict resolution, environmental protection, and local development, and later established what came to be known as the Mesa Técnica de Apoyo a Tambogrande. The Mesa Técnica provided the legal and technical arguments of the opposition campaign and helped organize the details of the referendum in its earliest stages.[8]

This network of NGOs worked to generate a campaign strategy that could appeal to a wider audience, seeking to connect the antimining protest of Tambogrande to the nation's cultural identity. The campaign focused on the national significance of limes and what they represented for a number of traditional staples of Peruvian cuisine, such as "ceviche" and "pisco sour." Tambogrande was one of the leading producers of limes, and thus an attack on the agricultural basin of Tambogrande endangered its production as well as Peru's cultural traditions. Lime-colored campaign signs and banners were posted throughout Lima. One of the posters, which was shown all over Lima, was composed of "the Peruvian flag with the names of popular lime-based dishes written across it, with some letters replaced by a lime, emphasiz[ing] the importance of the lime for national identity, without even mentioning Tambogrande directly" (Haarstad and Fløysand 2007, 302). Another slogan in the opposition campaign read, "there is no ceviche without limes" ("sin limón no hay ceviche"). This campaign was successful in creating a link between the grievances affecting Tambogrande and the country's traditions, boosting national solidarity on behalf of Tambogrande.

Transnationally, international NGOs, such as Oxfam America and Oxfam UK, provided financial and logistical resources to the local opposition and their support network of NGOs.[9] Oxfam UK, for instance, financed the referendum, spending approximately US $20,000 (Paredes 2008, 295). Although the direct influence that the referendum had on governmental decisions can be debated, without such financing, the referendum would have not taken place.

International NGOs also supported the preparation of parallel technical reports about the impact of mining. Oxfam America and Oxfam UK commissioned Dr. Robert Moran, a hydrologist and well-respected expert on the environmental impacts of mining, to write a report about the potential dangers that mining would pose for the surrounding ecosystem. Dr. Moran's report spelled out several of these threats. One was that open-pit mining, by its very nature, requires a large amount of water. MMC was public in its plans to divert some of the local tributaries of the Piura River, which would further strain limited water supplies. The increased demand for water needed for mining would drastically hurt agricultural exports. Another issue had to do with the toxic chemicals that are commonly involved in modern mining. Substances such as cyanide, kerosene, and acids are used to strip the minerals from the rock. Without the proper integrity of waste disposal facilities, the danger of contaminants seeping into the ground water and soil is a constant threat (Oxfam America 2001).[10] These environmental concerns involving the water supply and toxic chemicals were magnified by the fact that the MEM both owns a 25 percent stake in the company (through Centromín Perú) and also acts as regulator. Given this inherent conflict of interest, Dr. Moran, along with other observers, argued that MEM would not observe costly regulations that could cut into net profits and, therefore, government revenue.

Other international NGOs drew on the powerful frame of democracy. Because the national government did not recognize the outcome of the referendum, international NGOs felt the government was infringing on democratic principles of self-determination. International NGOs disseminated these developments through email lists, Web sites, and Internet news providers (Haarstad and Fløysand 2007). These outlets discussed the referendum and positioned the Tambogrande narrative within global struggles for democracy. These sites sent the message that the will of the community had been "ignored," and, therefore, something had to be done to address this problem (Haarstad and Fløysand 2007, 303). Several Web sites requested letters to be sent to President Toledo asking him to abandon the project.

To sum up, the arguments from aggrieved groups can be categorized into three distinct yet interconnected layers. First, there is the local region, at which residents fought the mine on the grounds that it was not compatible with agriculture. Second, at the national level, opposition leaders worked with mostly Lima-based NGOs establishing the Mesa Técnica and framed the issue as a battle over Peruvian identity, rather than solely Tambogrande's identity. Finally, transnationally, an international network of activists worked to frame the issue as an attack on democratic principles of self-determination. This network of scales was essential for the overall success of the opposition campaign.

The Response of "New Mining"

MMC and SNMPE—the leading mining business organization located in Lima—along with supporters of the mining industry in the government, mostly in the MEM, underestimated the resilience of the defense front and the vast network of NGOs that worked side by side with the front. In this section, I discuss the perceptions of the mining industry concerning the benefits of resource extraction in Tambogrande, as well as their views about the work of the NGOs that opposed mining.

Mining interests presented their position as one of providing economic development to a chronically poor region. The town of Tambogrande was falling behind the national and regional averages in several indicators of development. According to the 1993 census, for instance, 25.5 percent of the population was illiterate. Sewage treatment services only reached 66 percent of the town, and even more shocking, only 16 percent had access to potable water. Nearly 87 percent of the town did not have access to the national electric grid.[11] Despite the success of Tambogrande's agricultural exports, few other indicators demonstrated that the town was developing. Therefore, the future extraction of gold and copper in Tambogrande, in particular, meant improved socioeconomic conditions for its local residents and promised to enrich their lives.

In addition, resource extraction offered the potential to bring significant revenues to the national government's coffers. These revenues could then be devolved to the regions where extractive activities take place, such as Tambogrande, and thus provide for infrastructure development and educational and health services. Resource extraction could also provide for employment, which supporters presumed was likely to yield a higher income than agricultural cultivation. However, as discussed earlier, the town of Tambogrande, represented by the defense front, wanted none of the foreign capital offered. In the words of the late García Baca, whose assassination is still unresolved, "there is nothing to negotiate here" ("aquí no hay nada que negociar") (De Echave et al. 2009, 34).

With regard to the work of NGOs, mining interests believed these organizations simply stirred the pot, taking advantage of the raw emotions of local residents and using them to further their own publicity. Mining engineers mockingly portrayed environmental NGOs as "watermelons" (green on the outside but red inside) because they sought to protect the environment while preventing the spread of capitalism (Arellano-Yanguas 2008, 24). At one level, MMC and SNMPE argued that the reports prepared by NGOs exaggerated the threat of pollution from mining activities. In particular, the fears of environmental contamination did not address modern technologies that make it possible for mining to coexist with agriculture. These dangers, they argued, were presented as facts, which then were used in arguments in opposition to mining, even when no actual mining operations had taken place. However, these perceptions about the potential damage mining inflicts on environmental habitat are often well-ingrained into the psyche of the public and are difficult for the mining industry to rebut, given mining's already negative image because of previous cases of contamination and neglect in other areas. The mercury spill discussed in chapter 5 is such a case.

At another level, reflecting businesses' lack of empathy and elitism, the mining industry was insensitive to the calls for self-determination made by the FDVST on behalf of Tambogrande. The outcome of the referendum was questionable because it was paid for by an international NGO (Oxfam UK) with total disregard of the Peruvian laws that regulate productive activities. It encouraged disobedience of the rule of law (Paredes 2008, 296). However, by dismissing consultation rights, the mining industry inadvertently gave the impression that these demands came not from ordinary citizens, but rather from disaffected radicals who solely promoted disorder.

The Impact on Local Politics

As presented in chapter 3, in several protests like those in Tambogrande, residents, with the support of their local authorities, were quick to denounce the perceived collusion between mining companies and the central government in awarding mining claims and thus forged coalitions in opposition to mining. As in the 1980s, the ties between the local population and their political authorities were very strong, given that local leaders were also well-known and -established farmers who had eventually ventured into local politics. The start and end of the mobilization of Tambogrande crisscrosses two mayoral administrations. Each administration was greatly affected by the events of the conflict, becoming two of the opposition's greatest supporters.

The first administration, of Mayor Alfredo Rengifo Navarrete, elected in 1999 and serving until 2002, initially supported mining and extended MMC permission to begin its exploration activities. Mayor Rengifo wanted to know the mining potential of Tambogrande and planned to later decide whether mining had earned his full support or his opposition. However, the reports took several years to complete, and preliminary reports were constantly being challenged. During that period, the local opposition to MMC enlisted the support of a wider network of NGOs outside the town, and as the scale and intensity of contention grew, Mayor Rengifo's position also changed. He supported the popular referendum as a mechanism to learn exactly what the population of Tambogrande thought about MMC (De Echave 2009, 36). The results of the referendum, which overwhelmingly opposed mining, solidified his disagreement with the mining project. Overall, Mayor Rengifo's views about MMC evolved as the narrative of the conflict progressed.

By late 2002, a new mayoral administration promised to stop the mine completely, a promise that, given the record of the mayoral candidate, seemed very likely. The president of the defense front, Francisco Ojeda Riofrío, became the mayor of Tambogrande for the period 2003–6. Riofrío, previously a secondary school teacher and farmer, had worked his way up to the leadership of the defense front. While serving as mayor, he continued his functions as president of the defense front. Some critics said this showed a clear conflict of interest and devalued his role as a community leader interested solely in political goals. However, his supporters, greater in number, believed that his devotion to both positions demonstrated his strong commitment to the community and thus made him entirely trustworthy. In sum, the defense front and the municipal government of Tambogrande were one and the same, and in the long run these connections enhanced the chances of the opposition to mount an effective resistance against MMC.

Mayor Ojeda Riofrío has given several interviews describing the key events of the "battle" for Tambogrande. A couple of points about his role in these events are worth noting. First, he mentions offers from MMC to rebuild Tambogrande's local school, including painting it and purchasing computers, as well as opportunities to live abroad for him and his family. This strategy of bribing local leaders is very common, and it often works. But in this case, Mayor Ojeda Riofrío said no. As stated earlier, the presence of organizations with strong ties to the local community served as a check on leaders, like Mayor Ojeda Riofrío, and made the possible distribution of material rewards or other forms of cooptation ineffective. The relevance of preexisting organizations, such as producers' associations (asociaciones de productores) and water users' boards (junta de usuarios de riego), in constraining the actions of leaders should not be underestimated. As an illustration, and examining the role of the water users' boards in other mobilizations in northern Peru, Muñoz (2009, 96) writes that "the majority of farmer-members of these water users' boards know each other from the past; they have approached each other multiple times for different reasons, sometimes because of business opportunities and other times because of family or communal activities; they see each other during the town's celebrations or they have organized these festivities together; they go to the same restaurants or bars or shops to talk; and they also participate in the same parent-teachers conferences as other members of these boards."

Second, during the mobilizations in opposition to MMC, he mentions a defamation campaign by the local print media. For instance, El Correo, the conservative local newspaper that supported mining, printed a headline stating that "Pancho Ojeda was sightseeing in Europe" ("Pancho Ojeda se pasea por Europa"), while the mayor had in fact never visited the old continent (Paredes 2008, 290). In contrast, the town's other local newspaper, El Tiempo, sided with the defense front and ran several articles in favor of the environment and agriculture.

The "battle" for Tambogrande illustrates well the growing complexity of protest movements in Peru. The protest took place in the distant region of Piura in northern Peru, and like hundreds of protests elsewhere in the country, it appeared that the antimining protest against

MMC would remain a geographically isolated event. This was not the case. Instead protestors built and drew upon a large network of national and international NGOs and were able to successfully influence the government to rescind the mining rights that had been given to MMC. Protestors also presented a successful frame that resonated well with the national culture. Aside from tapping into the importance of limes to the country's identity, they also portrayed Tambogrande as the nation's "breadbasket." And both agrarian elites and local residents were eager to continue with this image (Olortegui 2007, 52). In this context, the case for development by extracting resources that would compromise the existing water supply and damage the agricultural basin was a difficult platform for MMC and the government to advance. In the end, Tambogrande's productive agricultural economy truncated the expansion of the extractive economy as represented by "new mining."

A couple of additional observations with relevance to other antimining mobilizations can be drawn from this case study. First, Tambogrande was the first protest to invoke a popular referendum in opposition to mining. This strategy, which was neither legally sanctioned nor authorized by the national government, has been replicated in other antimining protests in Peru, such as Tía María of Southern Corporation (in Arequipa) and Río Blanco of Minera Majaz (in Piura), and with the same political objective. In this way, Tambogrande shaped the repertoire of contention nationally. More generally, the referendum strategy highlights the range of options available for aggrieved groups under democracy. As explained earlier, in the early stages of the campaign, the defense front resorted to violent acts, yet as the opposition movement grew, the front became more strategic, organizing the referendum during the later stages of the campaign. Thus, confrontational, disruptive strategies (e.g., the destruction of MMC property) intertwined with assimilative and more traditional types of grassroots democracy (e.g., the referendum). This model of consultation has also emerged in other Latin American countries—a theme that I return to in the concluding chapter of this book.

Second, and finally, local politicians played a key role in the opposition campaign against MMC, even when parties were fluid and weak. Francisco Ojeda Riofrío led the defense front during the early stages of the campaign and later was elected the mayor of Tambogrande. He was voted into office opposing mining interests, and after his election, he fulfilled his campaign promises and put an end to MMC's mining rights. The presence of organizations with strong ties to the local community helped to mount an effective resistance against mining. Local leaders had better control of their organizations. These organizations also served as a check on leaders and made the distribution of material rewards and other forms of cooptation ineffective. The next chapter expands on these ideas for the case of Mount Quilish in Cajamarca.

CHAPTER 5

MINING MOUNTAINS

Since the turn of the twentieth century, agriculture and mining in the northern region of Cajamarca have coexisted rather peacefully. The region developed an agricultural economy with abundant dairy farms next to several small-scale mining operations, some of which were exploited informally. Starting in the early 1990s and continuing to this day, however, this peaceful coexistence came to a halt with the arrival of the Yanacocha mine. By the late 2000s, the mine had pulled more than nineteen million ounces of gold, worth approximately US $7 billion.[1] The mine is currently the largest gold producer in Latin America and one of the largest foreign investment operations in the country.

The Yanacocha mine has triggered several mobilizations resulting from a wide range of issues, such as environmental contamination, land use matters, water rights disputes, and so on. These events echo the truth of a history lesson reported recently in the *New York Times*: "where there is gold, there is conflict, and the more gold, the more conflict."[2] Generally, these mobilizations were sporadic and short-lived and remained largely localized. The aggrieved groups that were fighting Yanacocha had specific claims and failed to build larger coalitions in opposition to mining. The mobilizations reflected the fragmentation of organizations opposed to mining in Cajamarca, as well as the asymmetries in dealing with the second-largest gold producer in the world—Denver-based Newmont Mining Corporation, which controls most of Yanacocha.

However, the mobilization against the expansion of the mine in Mount Quilish (Cerro Quilish) in 2004 was an important exception. This mobilization crisscrossed the rural-urban divide, producing perhaps the largest demonstration in the history of Cajamarca. As in Tambogrande (chapter 4), the success of aggrieved groups rested on their organizational strength, as well as on an effective framing campaign in opposition to mining. Preexisting agricultural-based organizations coalesced into a larger opposition movement known as the Mount Quilish Defense Front (Frente de Defensa del Cerro Quilish). The front's strategic framing campaign, which presented a stark choice summarized as "water yes, gold no" ("agua sí, oro no"), helped to draw the support of other organizations throughout Cajamarca and produced high levels of collective action in opposition to mining. While the protest stopped the extraction of gold in this zone, Yanacocha's search for this mineral, buoyed by high prices, has moved to other areas.

I begin this chapter by tracing the expansion of the mine in the region. Then I discuss two key events that have shaped its trajectory in the area: the mobilization denouncing the mercury spill of Choropampa in 2000 and the mobilization against the expansion of the mine in Mount Quilish in 2004. Thereafter, I revisit the organizational and coalitional capacity of aggrieved groups that fought against Yanacocha, as these groups are widely perceived as weak and fragmented compared to other cases. The conclusion reexamines the impact of these mobilizations on national politics.

Yanacocha Moves In

Similar to Tambogrande (chapter 4), the arrival of Yanacocha clashed with the local agricultural economy. The earliest disputes with the mine had to do with the purchase of land, which most observers agree was undersold. Other disputes had to do with the contamination of water, by which small farmers living in lower-altitude areas were affected the most. These disputes, however, remained localized and geographically dispersed. Overlapping these problems, Yanacocha was immersed in its own legal battle over the control of the company. This legal battle was triggered when one foreign partner decided to sell its shares to another foreign company, denying the first right of refusal to existing partners. These problems damaged the company's public image and, as explained later, negatively affected the trajectory of the company in the region.

The Yanacocha mine began purchasing land in 1992, shortly after the company was first established. The acquisition of land split the rural area around Cajamarca. Those who lived in the higher-altitude areas felt that the sale of their land had been worth it, since the land was not as valuable for farming. However, most of the people who lived in the lower-altitude areas remained wary of the environmental effects the mining company's presence would have on their farmland (Meléndez 2009). Yanacocha negotiated with small farmers on an individual basis, rather than as a group. Several authors agree that it was unlikely that many knew whether they were receiving a good price for the land (Lingán 2008; De Echave et al. 2009). According to the Ecumenical Foundation for Development and Peace (Federación Ecuménica para el Desarrollo y la Paz, FEDEPAZ), the group of families who sold their land between 1992 and 1993 received an average of 100 to 200 Peruvian soles per hectare of land (US $46 to US $92 per 2.47 acres, respectively), which in the early 1990s represented the "market price" for their land (Lingán 2008, 42; Meléndez 2009, 327).

In 1993, the families who felt their land had been undersold approached the local political authorities to complain about Yanacocha and to demand a better, just price for their land. These petitions, however, did not have any real impact as they came from individual small farmers, and not a larger group of organized land owners. Then these families approached Father Marco Arana, a Catholic priest near the Río Porcón locality, which was one of the first areas affected by Yanacocha's purchase of land (Meléndez 2009, 327). Father Arana presided over the Training and Intervention Group for Sustainable Development (Grupo de Formación e Intervención para el Desarrollo Sostenible, GRUFIDES), an NGO that provided associational space for young activists to discuss environmental issues and support to communities affected by mining. On the locals' behalf, the Catholic Church filed complaints with the management at Newmont and the World Bank. The involvement of the World Bank had to do with its small ownership of the Yanacocha mine, as explained below. As a result of these petitions, Yanacocha agreed to negotiate with small farmers. The negotiations resulted in an increase in the initial prices paid for the small farmers' properties (Lingán 2008, 32). The claims of aggrieved farmers having been met, the disputes over the purchase of land dissipated.

Paralleling these land disputes and over a period of approximately seven years, the partners of the company went through a very complicated legal battle to establish their control of the mine. The original owners of Yanacocha included the US-based Newmont Mining Company (38.0 percent), the Peruvian firm Compañía de Minas Buenaventura (32.3 percent), the French state-owned company Bureau de Recherches Géologiques et Minières (BRGM) (24.7 percent), and the International Finance Corporation (IFC), a division of the World Bank (5 percent) (De Echave et al. 2009, 75). No partner had a controlling interest. Then in 1993 the French government decided to privatize BRGM, announcing its sale transfer to an Australian-based company, Normandy Poseidon (De Echave et al. 2009, 75). Both Newmont and Buenaventura objected to the transaction on the grounds of their first right of refusal on any sale among partners. Several years later, the Peruvian Supreme Court ruled in favor of Newmont and Buenaventura. Newmont then became the majority shareholder of Yanacocha (51.35 percent), followed by Buenaventura (43.65 percent) and the IFIC (5.00 percent). The Supreme Court decision, which came out in 1998, appeared to have settled the control of the company.

However, after the downfall of the Fujimori regime in late 2000, a videotape made by Fujimori's security chief Vladimiro Montesinos surfaced. This videotape, first broadcast in 2001, shows an exchange between Lawrence T. Kurlander, Newmont's number-three executive at that time, and Montesinos. Their meeting took place in February 1998. In the recording, Montesinos offers to help with the voting of the Supreme Court, and after this exchange, both Kurlander and Montesinos pledge friendship for life. "Now you have a friend for life," Kurlander tells Montesinos. "You have a friend for life also," Montesinos replies.[3] Another video, recorded in May 1998, shows a meeting between Montesinos and Supreme Court judge Jaime Beltrán Quiroga. In the recording, Montesinos advocates on behalf of Newmont, citing Peruvian national interests that he holds are at stake. Judge Beltrán would later play a crucial role in the case, as his vote would be the deciding vote in the Newmont victory.

In summary, starting with the low price given to the first group of small farmers in the early 1990s and including the alleged bribes in order to establish control of the company in the late 1990s, a cloud of public distrust hung over the Yanacocha mine. Yanacocha's poor handling of the mercury spill in Choropampa magnified these perceptions, and it would inadvertently complicate the plans of the company in the long run.

"La Mina Que No Contamina"

To better understand the environmental concerns surrounding Yanacocha, a brief overview of the open-pit mining process to extract gold may be necessary. The bits of gold located in Cajamarca are found near the surface and are so small that they are often referred to as "invisible" or "flour" gold. The gold is mined by blasting mountains. Then it is culled with vast quantities of cyanide diluted with vast quantities of water. This treatment of the gold ore, also known as the "cyanide leach process," requires settling ponds, where the water eventually evaporates. The toxicity of this aqueous solution of cyanide has the potential to negatively damage the surrounding environment, particularly the groundwater and surface water systems.[4]

The fears of environmental damage associated with the open-pit mining process have always been present, but Yanacocha had self-cultivated an institutional image as "the mine that does not contaminate" ("la mina que no contamina"). Similar to MMC (chapter 4), Yanacocha also argued that the fears of environmental contamination did not address modern technologies that make it possible for mining to coexist with other economic activities, such as agriculture. The mercury spill in the district of Choropampa in 2000, coupled with Yanacocha's poor handling of the accident, proved otherwise. The spill tarnished the company's public image and further threw into question its capacity to confront environmental disasters.

On June 2, 2000, a truck from RANSA, a transporting service subcontracted by Yanacocha, spilled approximately 151 kilograms of mercury onto a road. Toxic liquid mercury sheets broke into puddles along the twenty-five-mile stretch of highway. Locals started collecting the material, believing it to be of value because of its silvery metallic appearance. Curious children played with the liquid, even tasted it, unaware of the severe toxicity of the substance (Monning 2005).[5] An expeditious response from Yanacocha could have prevented the mercury from coming into contact with the local population. Such action, however, did not happen. In total, the spill affected more than three hundred people.

Instead, Yanacocha argued that they were not directly responsible for the spill, since those who were transporting the mercury worked for a subcontracted company—RANSA. Yanacocha then resorted to paying residents to collect the mercury on the highway for deposit in containers; however, locals were not given the proper protective clothing, gloves, or respirators. The response by political authorities was mixed. As one would expect, local authorities closer to the town demanded a solution, yet regional authorities representing Cajamarca, including officials of the central government led by Alberto Fujimori, tried to play down the accident. The latter group was arguably more interested in putting the issue to rest.

Led by Choropampa's mayor, Lot Saavedra, the local population denounced Yanacocha's indifference, as well as the central government's inaction. Mayor Saavedra organized a series of demonstrations, which eventually forced Yanacocha to negotiate with the locals in Choropampa. During the negotiations, the town's residents did not present a unified set of demands; rather, they voiced divided interests, while Yanacocha tried to be practical by giving in as little as possible. Yanacocha offered to provide limited health care coverage and a number of public works on behalf of the population (e.g., parks, sport facilities). It did not offer any kind of general compensation to the people affected by the spill. The locals reluctantly accepted Yanacocha's offer. Then the mobilizations over the spill faded away.

While the demonstrations in Choropampa remained localized, the events surrounding the mercury spill led to a number of important developments. Nationally, it sparked the creation of the first ecological organizations in the country, such as ECOVIDA (Asociación para la Defensa Ambiental de Cajamarca; Association for the Environmental Defense of Cajamarca) and ADEA (Asociación de Defensa y Educación Ambiental; Association of Defense and Environmental Education). These organizations brought together local environmental activists and sought to raise awareness of the environmental threats surrounding Yanacocha's presence in Cajamarca. Similarly, the first local committees in defense of the environment were created in the provinces of Cajamarca, San Pablo, Celendín, and Bambamarca (Meléndez 2009,

331–32). The spill was also covered in the local print media. As in the case of Tambogrande, one local newspaper (*Clarín*) sided with Yanacocha and minimized the scale of the accident. The other local newspaper (Panorama) was more environmentally conscious and thus more critical of Yanacocha. Outside the country, the Choropampa mercury spill put Yanacocha in the international spotlight, as several international NGOs, like Oxfam UK, became interested in monitoring the effects of the mine.

Overall, the Choropampa mercury spill acted as a catalyst in the community, sparking suspicion about Yanacocha's safety standards and the effects of its operations on the environment (De Echave et al. 2009, 83–84). It shed light on its inability (and perhaps unwillingness) to address the claims of local communities. Following the spill, smaller incidents that had previously gone unnoticed were now more carefully scrutinized. For instance, one involved the death of hundreds of trout in nearby Río Llaucano and resulted in a roadblock on the Cajamarca-Bambamarca road for one whole week (De Echave et al. 2009, 84). Another involved the alleged presence of solid mercury in the main water pipes of the city, which spurred a citywide mobilization led by the provincial mayor of Cajamarca, Jorge Hoyos Rubio. For the locals, it did not matter whether Yanacocha was directly responsible for these events, as in the case of the dead trout, or whether the events were factual, as in the case of mercury found in the water pipes of the city. Perceptions shaped the locals' reality. The distrust toward Yanacocha had grown to a boiling point. It clearly began to overshadow the economic benefits of mining for the region.

Mining Mountains

Up until now, the majority of protests in opposition to Yanacocha had been sporadic and had remained localized. The claims against the mine were specific and affected geographically dispersed towns, mostly rural. The groups of protestors participating in these mobilizations also did not coalesce into a broader, regional coalition in opposition to mining. The mobilization against the expansion of the mine into Mount Quilish, in contrast, brought together thousands of protestors from various sectors of civil society (e.g., small farmers, university students, unions, etc.) and across diverse provinces throughout Cajamarca. The protest crisscrossed the rural-urban divide and produced one of the largest mobilizations in the history of Cajamarca. The Mount Quilish Defense Front (Frente de Defensa del Cerro Quilish) emerged as the leading antimining coalition against Yanachocha. The front's strategic framing campaign, articulating that water was more precious than gold, was instrumental for aggrieved groups to build both associational power and collective power and produced very high levels of collective action. Protestors fought for water rights against Yanacocha with memes, such as "water yes, gold no" ("agua sí, oro no") and "life yes, gold no" ("vida sí, oro no"), and successfully derailed the expansion of the mine into the region. Similar to the other case studies in this book, the political environment following the collapse of the Fujimori regime was also more favorable to mobilization.

Below I describe the key events that led to this large-scale mobilization. Similar to Tambogrande (chapter 4) and Bagua (chapter 6), the mobilizations in Quilish mixed street protests (e.g., roadblocks) with more peaceful forms of dispute resolution (e.g., judicial review, bargaining roundtables, etc.). In these mobilizations, typically, aggrieved groups approach their local authorities (e.g., mayors) first to protest against extraction, though sometimes mayors themselves lead the protests against mining. Other political authorities, like regional politicians, are more opportunistic and join the protests much later, once they have seen evidence of widespread social opposition to extraction. In all of these cases, it appears that the intensity of mobilizations is inversely related to the exhaustion of possible venues or channels to challenge extraction. But as discussed later, the ability of institutional channels to resolve disputes has less to do with their presence or absence and more to do with their ability to produce politically binding commitments.

Quilish before the September 2004 Outburst

La Quinua and El Quilish are two mountains separated by the Río Grande, the main water source for Cajamarca. Yanacocha began its activities in the area around La Quinua but soon became interested in moving to the Quilish area. Yanacocha had located at least 3.7 million ounces of gold in Quilish, which would extend the life of mining operations in the region. In addition, the price of gold was rising quickly. It went from US $280 per troy ounce in 2000 to US $410 in 2004 and to US $1222 in 2010 (see figure 6). However, the locals did not want Quilish to be the center of any mining activity because it was thought of as an "aquiferous cushion" ("colchon acuífero"), or a hill made of permeable rock which supplied about 70 percent of the town's water. Residents were afraid that drilling into the hill would diminish the community's water supply. In brief, Yanacocha wanted more gold, but the locals wanted to protect the town's water supply. The choice between gold and water summarizes well the mobilization in Mount Quilish.

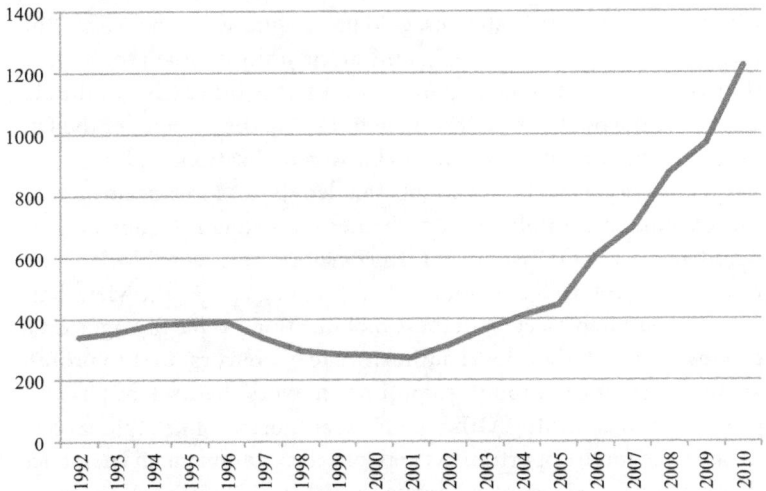

FIGURE 6. Gold prices ($US per troy ounce). *Source*: MEM 2004, 2010.

Anticipating that Yanacocha might want to explore the area around Quilish, in October 2000, four months after the Choropampa mercury spill, Mayor Hoyos Rubio issued an ordinance declaring the area around Quilish a protected reserve. By passing ordinance 012–2000, the local government was exercising its power to decide how the land in its jurisdiction would be used. While the ordinance was well received by the local population, it began a legal tug-of-war between local authorities who opposed Yanacocha and representatives of the central government who supported mining (and Yanacocha).

Yanacocha fought ordinance 012 in the courts. The company initially lost at the first two levels of appeal. However, in April 2003, the Peruvian Constitutional Tribunal (Tribunal Constitucional, TC) ultimately ruled in favor of the mine. The TC argued that Mayor Hoyos Rubio had the authority to issue ordinances, but in this particular case the ordinance was invalid because it had been made after the central government gave Yanacocha its mining concession rights. The TC did ask Yanacocha to present an environmental impact report (estudio de impacto ambiental, EIA). Following the TC decision, in July 2004 the MEM authorized Yanacocha to move forward with exploration at Quilish. It gave Yanacocha a permit known as "type C" through Board Resolución 361 (Resolution Directorial 361).

The Outburst

Since the time of ordinance 012 in 2000 until the extension of Board Resolution 361 in 2004, several mobilizations took place in "defense of Quilish" (Meléndez 2009, 340).[6] These mobilizations were coordinated by the Mount Quilish Defense Front, which brought together environmental activists, rural patrols (*rondas campesinas*), and other leaders of NGOs opposed to mining (Meléndez 2009, 337). Iván Salas, a former militant of the Peruvian left, was the leader of the front. But the initial response to the calls for mobilizations was weak. The bulk of political leaders and regional authorities representing Cajamarca stayed out of the conflict. In fact, Cajamarca's first regional president, Luis Pita, and the new provincial mayor of Cajamarca, Emilio Horna (replacing Hoyos Rubio, who had issued ordinance 012), came from APRA, and they both supported Yanacocha's incursion into Mount Quilish (De Echave et al. 2009, 86–87).

Backed by Board Resolution 361, Yanacocha began to transport its machinery to Quilish. The mine also heightened its own security, both privately and with help from the national police. In the view of the local population, all the possible legal venues to challenge Yanacocha were now closed or simply exhausted. The TC sided with Yanacocha. The MEM gave the green light to start explorations. The TC and the MEM came to decisions that supported mining, but mobilizations continued because these decisions were simply not binding for the locals. Moreover, their political leaders, like regional president Pita and provincial mayor Horna, suggested that they did not have legal authority in a case this large. It was then that the prefect of Cajamarca, Carlos Alarcón, stepped in to coordinate a meeting between the locals and representatives of MEM. Specifically, they would meet with the general director of environmental and mining matters of the MEM, Julio Bonelli, and Felipe Quea, an advisor of the MEM. An initial meeting was set for August 16, 2004, and a follow-up meeting would take place shortly after, on August 26. At the first meeting, according to the local population, the MEM representatives offered to resolve the ongoing dispute with Yanacocha. On the date of the follow-up meeting, however, the MEM representatives did not show up. The MEM, instead, sent out a statement that no definitive answer had been made and that a meeting without an answer from Lima would be fruitless. The locals were furious. Protest leaders promised to fight to the death to defend Mount Quilish and planned a demonstration for September 2 to "recuperate Mount Quilish" (Meléndez 2009, 342).[7]

At 10 a.m. on September 2, 2004, approximately two thousand small farmers answered the call and arrived at Quilish to protest the explorations of Yanacocha. Similar to Tambogrande (chapter 4), the agricultural economy by its very definition made available a range of preexisting organizations, such as producers' associations (asociaciones de productores) and water users' boards (junta de usuarios de riego), upon which sustained mobilizations could develop. The leaders behind the September 2 mobilization were representatives of water users' boards, like the microbasin of Río Grande and the microbasin of Río Porcón. As pointed our earlier, the area of Porcón was the first affected by the purchase of land by Yanacocha, and it was where Father Arana worked as a pastor. Gomer Vargas, the mayor of Huambocancha, emerged as a mediator between these organizations and political authorities in the city (Meléndez 2009, 344–45).[8]

The company requested intervention by the national police, which immediately sent 120 officers to the area in both cars and helicopters to break up the demonstration. They employed tear gas, and the ensuing confrontation ended with dozens of casualties on both sides. Protestors took the intervention of the government as an example of excessive use of force, engendering further confrontation. Around 4 p.m. on the same day, the remaining protestors left the site, heading to a roadblock on the Cajamarca-Bambamarca road that had been set up earlier by another group. Yanacocha had heightened security and was able to end the protest quickly. However, the locals were growing more frustrated at Yanacocha's mistreatment (Meléndez 2009, 343; De Echave et al. 2009, 90).

News of the September 2 conflict spread quickly to the capital. A clash between a multinational company with the national police behind them and a group of small farmers appeared uneven. The perception of excessive use of force by the government caught the attention of some urban organizations that would later come to the aid of the small farmers. The following day (September 3), newspapers printed headlines such as "Small Farmers Massacred by Police" ("Campesinos son masacrados por la policía") (Meléndez 2009, 344).

After the incident at Quilish, the protestors moved to the roadblock, only to encounter the police once more, resulting in many more detainments and casualties. On the morning of September 3, having seen the headlines and heard about the violent clash between protestors and police, hundreds of university students and young activists came to the area. They decided to go to the water treatment facility known as El Milagro, which was near the roadblock, and close the valves, cutting off the city's water supply. In solidarity with the small farmers, their objective was to "show Cajamarca what it felt like being without water" (Meléndez 2009, 344). With the participation of university students and their actions, the mobilization crossed the rural-urban divide and would grow even more.

On September 6, a commission was sent from Lima to find a solution to the mobilization in Quilish. The meeting took place in Cajamarca, and access to the public was restricted to avoid disruptions. In attendance were MEM representatives (Julio Bonelli and Felipe Quea), Yanacocha employees, police authorities, Father Marco Arana, Elena Sánchez of the Mesa de Concertación de Lucha Contra la Pobreza (MCLCP) (discussed later), and around eight local leaders representing water users' boards. Father Marco Arana explained that the protesting population would not retreat until the resolution allowing Yanacocha to explore was repealed. Legally, however, a repeal of the resolution was not possible; the most that could happen was a procedural suspension. This position, of course, was meant to protect Yanacocha's rights and to make good on the government's concessions to Yanacocha. In a word, if a roadblock could roll back a mining concession, that process would negatively affect investors' confidence elsewhere in the country. Although these legal arguments were clear to the leaders at the meeting, they were not as easily understood by the rest of the local population that was maintaining the blockade. State authorities were sent to the site of the roadblock on the Cajamarca-Bambamarca to attempt to explain the situation to those present. Although the group did not say much, they quickly observed the indignation of the protestors. The authorities promised to come back later that day, but they did not, thus creating a situation similar to that on August 26, when the MEM representatives (Julio Bonelli and Felipe Quea) did not return to Cajamarca for their follow-up visit. With protestors having been disappointed by the national government once again, the organized resistance continued (Meléndez 2009, 341–42; Echave et al. 2009).

For the first time since the beginning of the conflict, the regional president, Luis Pita, and the provincial mayor of Cajamarca, Emilio Horna, came to the Quilish area. Departing from their previous position, Pita and Horna signed an act that included seven points; among them was the repeal of Board Resolution 361. At this juncture, the mining company agreed to temporarily suspend its operations at Quilish and to begin studies analyzing the quantity of water resources in Quilish. Yanacocha's move was seen as a sign that the company was willing to negotiate with the locals in Quilish. However, showing the resilience of aggrieved groups, along with the government's passive response, the locals would not accept anything other than a full-fledged repeal of Board Resolution 361 by the central government.

On September 7, the defense front called for a regional strike the following day—September 8. Protestors marched to the departmental capital to demand that the MEM repeal Board Resolution 361. Reflecting mounting local pressure, now–provincial mayor Emilio Horna called for an indefinite strike until Board Resolution 361 was repealed (De Echave et al. 2009, 91; Meléndez 2009, 347–48). About ten thousand citizens joined the strike. Clearly at this point the mobilization was no longer limited to a group of small farmers representing the microbasins of Río Grande and Río Porcón.

By the end of the first week of protests, the conflict had created a national stir. On September 8, the Peruvian Congress came forward in an effort to find a solution to the mobilization. The chair of the Committee on Energy and Mines (Comisión de Energía y Minas), Luis Heysen Zegarra (APRA), appointed three congressional representatives to travel to Cajamarca and there organize a meeting with the participation of everyone involved in the dispute. The congressional representatives were: José Carrasco Távara (APRA), José Luis Devéscovi Dzierzón (FIM), and Edgar Villanueva (Perú Ahora). The roadblock on the Cajamarca-Bambamarca road continued. The venues to challenging Yanacocha that appeared to be closed or exhausted began to open again.

Starting in the second and final week of the protest (from September 9 until September 15), protestors formed a group known as Sole Civic Committee for the Defense of Life and the Environment (Comité Cívico Unitario para la Defensa de la Vida y del Medio Ambiente) to better coordinate their responses to the MEM and Yanacocha. Luis Salas, the leader of the defense front, become the coordinator of this Comité Cívico. Father Arana also played an active role during these negotiations. Reflecting the rural-urban divide previously mentioned, the discussions would take place in the city, and then a representative of the Comité Cívico (e.g., Father Arana) would be sent to the Cajamarca-Bambamarca roadblock to deliver the news to the group of small farmers stationed there. The sticking point during the negotiations was what to do with Board Resolution 361. Yanacocha was satisfied with its temporary suspension. Any other concessions beyond that would imply the potential loss of those 3.7 million ounces of gold estimated to be present in Mount Quilish. The protestors, in contrast, wanted its complete repeal. The MEM tried to come up with a solution that would satisfy both parties. It suspended Board Resolution 361 but added that the resolution was "without executive effect" ("sin efecto ejecutorio"). The suspension was valid until new environmental studies were conducted to examine how extractive activities would affect the city's access to water. These studies would be paid for by Yanacocha. Aggrieved groups said no to what appeared to be a "legalism" designed to diffuse the protest in the short term, while protecting Yanacocha's rights in the long run.

On September 15, a department-wide strike took place, as no formal agreement had been made. The strike was the combined effort of a multiplicity of organizations and actors, including university students, teachers, unions like CGTP, and rural patrols (rondas campesinas), among others. Approximately forty thousand people participated in roadblocks and mobilizations throughout the thirteen provinces of Cajamarca. The scale of the protest was unprecedented in the history of Cajamarca. In Choropampa, the site of the mercury spill, the police engaged protestors with tear gas and rubber bullets. The department-wide strike also paralyzed Yanacocha. The director of

Compañía de Minas Buenaventura (Newmont's partner), Roque Benavides, announced that Yanacocha would resume operations when security conditions had been reestablished in the area (Meléndez 2009, 351).

On September 16, the MEM published Board Resolution 427, which repealed Board Resolution 361 and blocked Yanacocha from continuing explorations in Mount Quilish. The new resolution was delivered by the minister of energy and mines, Jaime Quijandría. That night, the strike was lifted. On November 3, Yanacocha published a full-page announcement in the major newspapers of the country stating its decision to end exploration of Mount Quilish (Lingán 2008, 54). Yanacocha also acknowledged its mistakes in developing its relations with the population in Cajamarca.

Cajamarca's Associational and Collective Power

Generally, the mobilizations up until Quilish show evidence of associational power (i.e., organizational capacity). Existing organizations were recast, while new organizations were formed. Water users' boards, for instance, served as the ground floor in support of the defense front. In addition to associational power, the mobilization in Quilish also provides evidence of collective power (i.e., coalitional capacity), as rural-based organizations forged coalitions with urban-based ones. The mobilization in defense of Mount Quilish thus resulted in a process known as "scale-shift" (McAdam, Tarrow, and Tilly 2001), in which scattered and disarticulated instances of protest transform into growing streams of mobilization. Quilish, therefore, was an "upward scale-shift," from the local to the regional level, that came about as a consequence of the threat that mining posed to the town's water supply.[9]

The Quilish experience, however, was more the exception than the rule. Elsewhere in Cajamarca, the organizations that opposed mining are more fragmented in comparison to other cases, and the mobilizations there remain localized and territorially dispersed. Meléndez (2009) goes so far as to discuss the protests surrounding Yanacocha as a "mobilization without movements." In several of these mobilizations, aggrieved groups and the Yanacocha mine agreed to negotiate their differences by establishing a bargaining roundtable (mesa de diálogo) and then settled by signing a deed of commitment (acta de compromiso). Mining operations were sometimes interrupted while negotiations take place, but resumed once a settlement had been reached. For this reason, a stop-and-go pattern characterizes the extraction of gold in Cajamarca (see chapter 1, table 1). The fact that mining continues, despite repeated localized opposition, also reflects the asymmetries in dealing with a very large company, as well as the "structural" importance of gold extraction for the Peruvian economy. Gold exports were rising in the late 1990s and increased even more prior to Quilish (see figure 7). In all, Yanacocha was a key mega extractive project (megaproyecto minero), which was championed unequivocally by the central government.

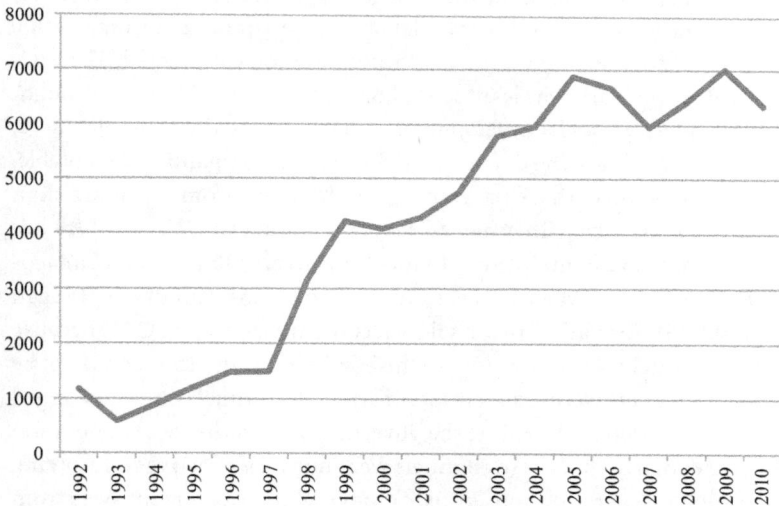

FIGURE 7. Volume of gold exports (in thousands troy ounces). *Source*: MEM 2004, 2010.

Exemplifying Cajamarca's organizational capacity, three different bargaining roundtables appeared during the first decade of the 2000s: CTAR (Transitional Regional Board), CAO (Compliance Advisor Ombudsman from the World Bank's IFC), and MCLCP (Roundtable for Poverty Reduction) (Meléndez 2009; Lingán 2009).[10] These roundtables drew a large number of civil society organizations (e.g., environmental NGOs like Ecovida and GRUFIDES, rondas campesinas, the Mount Quilish Defense Front, unions like CGTP and UNAC, etc.); representatives of diverse agencies of the central government, but mostly the MEM; regional and local political authorities of Cajamarca; and, last but not least, representatives of Yanacocha.

These bargaining roundtables were meant to provide a space to discuss the problems between the locals and Yanacocha and to later identify solutions on a consensual basis. In response to petitions from the local population, CTAR and CAO produced two environmental assessment reports of the area. These reports were subcontracted to outside agencies—INGETEC and Stratus Consulting, respectively. CAO's report, released in 2003, confirmed the contamination of the water close to the Yanacocha mine. These findings were read differently by those participating in the roundtable. Aggrieved groups, for instance, took these findings as testimonial of their resistance to mining, while Yanacocha understood them as a situation to be corrected. The MC-LCP, in contrast, was less focused on environmental issues. It sought to articulate a social development plan for the province of Cajamarca. However, Yanacocha did not participate in this bargaining roundtable.

On balance, these bargaining roundtables promised more than they could deliver. They had an easy entry (and exit). When CTAR addressed the intangibility of Mount Quilish, for instance, both Yanacocha and the MEM withdrew from the bargaining roundtable (Lingán 2008, 48). Similarly, other civil society organizations left CAO because they thought it was too close to the World Bank and thus could not be trusted. There were arguably lots of available channels that encouraged dialogue among the mine, the government, and the local population of Cajamarca, but these channels were not very effective in resolving disputes, generating consensus, or moving the government away from its passive stance. The bargaining roundtables shared the limitations of the decisions from the TC and the MEM in support of mining, inasmuch as they also produced results that were not politically binding.

The Aftermath of Quilish

The mobilizations surrounding Yanacocha have had substantive effects on national policies, requiring mining companies and the government to address more directly the social problems of the communities affected by mining. Three sets of ramifications are worth discussing. First, the social turmoil generated by the mercury spill, as well as the various mobilizations as a result of land use matters and water rights disputes with Yanacocha, set off a larger discussion concerning the social responsibility (or "social license") of extractive companies. Tellingly, when Yanacocha arrived in Cajamarca, the existing laws required mining companies to first conduct an EIA before the start of a project. The MEM would then approve these environmental impact reports. In addition to conducting an EIA, mining companies are now required to present a social responsibility plan that outlines how their operations will affect the development of the area where the mineral resource is extracted. Because this plan requires the approval of the local community, mining companies negotiate these plans with the community ahead of time. The evidence from Cajamarca suggests that sporadic and short-lived mobilizations, which at first sight may appear to be inconsequential, have forced companies like Yanacocha to build a better rapport with local communities over land and water rights, even while extraction continues in other areas. Social responsibility plans are a means to that end.[11]

Second, the increased demands for social responsibility projects have also resulted in changes in policy making to finance such programs from the state. As noted in chapter 3, the canon minero became the primary tax vehicle to redistribute the profits of extractive companies. In the early 2000s, the distribution of the canon minero went through additional changes to devolve greater revenues to the localities where natural resources were extracted.[12] Mobilizations like Quilish moved policy makers to support these changes in the allocation of revenues. For instance, in the final days of the regional strike in Mount Quilish, when Minister of Energy and Mines Jaime Quijandría arrive in the city to deliver Board Resolution 427, he gave a speech in which he acknowledged that the government "was guilty" ("es el culpable") for failing to devolve revenues that come from mining extractive activities.

Finally, returning to the contentious politics literature, the lack of regular access to institutions is often invoked to explain the use of protest. The evidence from Cajamarca, however, suggests that the association between protest and the lack of regular access to institutions is more complex than it appears. Cajamarca has a rich tradition of societal organizations (e.g., rondas campesinas). The events prior to the mobilization in Mount Quilish led to the formation of three separate bargaining roundtables, pulling in a wide range of grassroots organizations. Representatives of the executive and legislative branches of the government also followed the events in Quilish in an effort to resolve the dispute. In sum, plenty of institutional outlets were available. However, these institutional outlets failed to deliver politically binding commitments. Thus the relationship between protest and institutions is better understood in terms of the quality of institutions—how individuals are effectively represented by existing institutions and whether accountability and responsiveness can be established from these institutions. As seen in chapter 3, the multiparty environment found at the regional level advances several outlets for political representation (ENP is greater than 5), but these outlets are occupied by politicians who follow their "naked ambitions" and parties that lack programmatic, collective projects (Levitsky 2013). In the end, the limitations of these institutional outlets compromise both the quality of representation and the performance of subnational governments.

CHAPTER 6

BLOOD IN THE JUNGLE

In 2006, the United States and Peru signed a free trade agreement (FTA). The US-Peru FTA came on the heels of several years of macroeconomic stability, the arrival of mega extractive projects like Yanacocha's gold mine and Camisea's natural gas project, and last but not least a commodity export boom. The FTA was seen as a protective shield for the economic liberalization policies of the 1990s. The agreement was set to enter into full force in early 2009. To facilitate the conditions laid down in the FTA, the Peruvian Congress, dominated by the alliance between APRA and Fujimori's AF (Alianza para el Futuro), granted President García the authority to legislate by decree. In early 2008, the executive issued ninety-nine decrees, twelve of which opened the Amazon region for development.

García's expansion of the extractive frontier clashed with the ethnic indigenous federation AIDESEP (Asociación Interétnica de Desarrollo de la Selva Peruana; the Interethnic Development Association of the Peruvian Rainforest). Unlike the agriculture-based organizations described in the previous chapters, AIDESEP's ability to mount an effective resistance campaign drew instead on the cultural identity of the peoples who have inhabited the Amazon for generations. Two major mobilizations unfolded between 2008 and 2009; their chief objective was to repeal the decrees that opened the Amazon for exploration and extraction. In the mobilization of June 2009 in the province of Bagua, the confrontation with the police, following orders to diffuse the protest, resulted in the deaths of thirty-three individuals, all of them on the same day. Shortly after the Baguazo, as the indigenous mobilization against the opening of the Amazon came to be known, the decrees were forever suspended.

I begin this chapter by discussing García's policy initiatives that sought to expand the extractive economy, which also exemplify the deepening of economic liberalization policies as a consequence of growing volumes of foreign and domestic investment in the natural resource sector. As discussed below, President García emerged as an unequivocal champion of extractive activities and used the stature and publicity of the executive office to promote these policies. Next I explain the main sources of opposition to these policies, highlighting the role of AIDESEP as well as other organizations. After summarizing the key events of the mobilization, which unlike the previous cases did not involve a specific mining company, but rather the García government itself, I discuss its consequences for national politics.[1] AIDESEP not only rolled back the decrees but also successfully pushed the national government to recognize their long-awaited consultation rights. As in the previous chapters, and contradicting the conventional wisdom that downplays the effects of territorialized mobilizations, the Baguazo is another example showing how a localized, segmented outburst is likely to produce substantive gains for aggrieved groups.

Dog in the Manger Syndrome

The opening of the Amazon represented a new reach for economic liberalization policies because extractive activities up until then had expanded mostly in the coastal areas and highlands of the country. For instance, according to CooperAcción, an NGO that monitors mining concessions in the country, roughly 7.30 percent (9,840,415 hectares) of the national territory was under concession in 2005 (CooperAcción 2005). This percentage increased almost threefold to 19.64 percent (24,988,219 hectares) in 2011 (CooperAcción 2011). Yet concessions in the Amazon region were not very visible.

García championed businesses' agendas and markets, arguably more so than Fujimori in the 1990s. Several authors took note of García's new promarket discourse. For instance, Monge, Viale, and Bedoya (2011, 300) characterized his economic policies as a form of "radicalized, almost fundamentalist, neoliberalism." Others went on to liken President García's role to that of the president of CONFIEP (Confederación Nacional de Instituciones Empresariales Privadas;

the National Confederation of Private Business Institutions), Peru's business umbrella association, created in 1984 (M. García 2011, 203).[2] "Peru Goes Forward" ("El Peru Avanza") became the mantra of his government (M. García 2011). Describing the change from his statist policies from the 1980s, John Crabtree wrote: "Ideologically he has pirouetted around 180 degrees."[3]

In a series of editorials, published in *El Comercio* between October and December of 2007, García outlined his desire to extend investment's reach to the country's geological endowments.[4] He expressed his frustration with indigenous peoples, proclaiming that native rural communities and small landowners were an impediment to the efficient use of natural resources. Indigenous people were holding back other groups from extracting resources in the region. The first article in the series, entitled "Dog in the Manger Syndrome" ("El síndrome del perro del hortelano"), clearly stated the president's way of thinking but also kindled resentment among indigenous peoples. The title refers to a commonly used phrase describing someone who deprives others from something that they themselves have access to but are not using.[5] The other editorials that followed went on to describe how to resolve this impasse.

"There are many unused resources that cannot be traded, that do not receive investment and do not create jobs," President García wrote. "And all this because of the taboo of already past ideologies, idleness, laziness or the law of the dog in the manger that says, 'If I do not do it, then let no one do it.'" President García continued:

> When I visit the city of Ilo and I see its urban development, the most advanced in Peru, I know that it is the product of mining and fisheries, and it hurts to compare this with the town of Ayabaca, which has more mineral resources than the Cuajone mine in the south and yet lives in great poverty. And it is because the old anticapitalist communist of the nineteenth century dresses up as the protectionist in the twentieth century and changes his colors again in the twenty-first century to that of an environmentalist. But it is always anticapitalist, against investment, without explaining how, with poor farming, the leap can be made to greater development.[6]

In response to García's unabashed discourse in support of extraction, an editorial in *El Comercio* welcomed his "doctrinal maturity" ("maduración doctrinal"), which was markedly different from the "impetuousness of youth" ("ímpetu juvenil") evidenced by the García of the late 1980s. The editorial then urged the government to assume the responsibility to promote private investment in the country "wholesale" ("en forma generalizada").[7]

To sum up, García sought to steer the country deeper into economic liberalization. He encouraged the growth of big business, mostly foreign, to continue the country's rapid economic development. His desire to expand the extractive economy by decree to ease the implementation of the US-Peru FTA, however, was problematic. It reinforced what scholars have long characterized as the exclusionary governing practices of neoliberalism, which elsewhere in the region served to unleash various episodes of antimarket contention (Silva 2009). In the Peruvian case, however, the passage of the decrees did not precede an economic crisis. Rather they were issued in the context of an economic boom driven by high mineral commodity prices and China's aggressive demand for raw materials. More important, the political scenario was remarkably different from the Fujimori years. Similar to the previous cases (chapters 4 and 5), the events of Bagua unfolded in a context of greater political liberalization, with a livelier and freer press. The political environment was thus more favorable for AIDESEP to undertake collective action.

AIDESEP's Demands for Rights

Returning to the classification of protests presented in chapter 1, some protests against the extraction of natural resources entail "demands for services," while others comprise "demands for rights." The former are not necessarily antiextraction, but rather seek a better distribution of a town's geological wealth. These mobilizations are more likely to remain geographically localized because the claims of aggrieved groups are very specific and somewhat easier to satisfy. In contrast, the latter are opposed to extraction and are motivated by environmental concerns in defense of the water supply or the protection of lands. The mobilizations involving "demands for rights" have broader claims that are also more difficult to accommodate. These mobilizations are thus more likely to affect national politics. The Baguazo is such a case.

AIDESEP was the principal indigenous rights' organization behind the opposition protests against the opening of the Amazon.[8] Created in the 1970s, AIDESEP is made up of fifty-seven federations and territorial organizations, representing approximately 350,000 indigenous people across 1,350 different communities. AIDESEP is also a member of COICA (Coordinadora de las Organizaciones Indígenas de la Cuenca Amazónica; the Coordinator of Indigenous Organizations of the Amazon Basin), which is a regional organization representing indigenous populations from Peru, Ecuador, Bolivia, Colombia, Venezuela, Brazil, Guyana, French Guiana, and Suriname.[9]

The sources of dispute between AIDESEP and the García government were twofold. First, the decrees that opened the Amazon for development threatened the physical land, and in this manner they threatened the cultural identity of peoples who have dwelled on the Amazon for generations. The bulk of the decrees, in fact, sought to eliminate the collective ownership of lands (also known as communal lands), thus easing their commercialization on the basis of property rights and markets. A political cartoon printed in Lucha Indígena (2009) summarizes well the discrepancies between AIDESEP and President García. The cartoon shows a group of indigenous people speaking with García, who is sitting behind the wheels of a bulldozer. The indigenous leader says, "For us, development is solidarity, equality, and balanced management of resources." President García then responds, "How ignorant! Development means to extract petroleum and cut down forests to produce ethanol."[10]

Consistent with the discourse of the "Dog in the Manger Syndrome," García viewed the Amazon region as simply a natural resource waiting to be exploited. However, for the indigenous groups represented by AIDESEP, the Amazon was much more than that. Land and cultural identity were closely tangled. In the words of former president of AIDESEP Gil Inoach, "Without their land, indigenous people will lose their culture because the identity of indigenous people is linked to the land."[11] Other statements made by indigenous leaders reinforced the importance of the land to their cultural identity. For instance, Mario Palacios, president of CONACAMI (Confederación Nacional de Comunidades del Perú Afectadas por la Minería; the National Confederation of Peruvian Communities Affected by Mining), declared that "development should be in harmony with Mother Earth ... not destroy it." Similarly, Awajún Indian leader Salomon Aguanash stated that the indigenous population rejected the kind of development sponsored by García "because it [was] not sustainable and it threaten[ed] the Amazon rainforest, humanity's heritage" (quoted in Stetson 2010, 4). At the height of the indigenous mobilization, the president of AIDESEP, Alberto Pizango, stated: "We will die defending our land."[12]

A second source of dispute, arguably more important than the first one, involved the lack of prior consultation concerning the passage of those legislative decrees (*decretos legislativos*, DL). Based on AIDESEP, these consultation rights originated in Convention 169 (C169) from the International Labor Organization (ILO), which was ratified by Peru in 1994. C169 states that "in cases in which the State retains the ownership of mineral or sub-surface resources or rights to other re-sources pertaining to lands, governments shall establish or maintain procedures through which they shall consult these peoples, with a view to ascertaining whether and to what degree their interests would be prejudiced, before undertaking or permitting any programs for the exploration or exploitation of such resources pertaining to their lands."

C169 was not necessarily an act of window dressing. The creation of the Ichigkat-Muja Condor Mountain Range National Park in 2004 is one example of successful consultation with the indigenous popu-lation exercised by the Peruvian government. Through meetings with a number of indigenous communities, the government extended the national reserve created in 1999, from 863,277 hectares to 1,642,567 hectares. Its name was also changed from Condor Mountain Range National Park to the indigenous name Ichigkat-Muja Condor Moun-tain Range National Park (Lombardi 2010, 130–35). However, the same level of consultation was not exercised in the passage of those ninety-nine legislative decrees in 2008, especially the twelve decrees that AIDESEP opposed.

The Mobilizations

The mobilizations against the García government began in the months following the passage of the legislative decrees. In August 2008, AIDESEP organized a strike demanding their repeal, in particular DL 1015 and DL 1073. These decrees allowed for the commercializa-tion of communal lands and consequently threatened the integrity of indigenous land (see table 8). Indigenous protestors blocked the bridge Corral Quemado, located on the border between the Amazo-nas and Cajamarca regions, restricting access to passing vehicles. They set on fire a regional government building near the Madre de Dios

River and captured some of the vessels of Argentine oil company Plus Petrol close to the Urubamba River. On the eighth day of protests, a confrontation broke out between police and protestors in Aramango (thirty-seven miles from Bagua), resulting in twelve injuries—eight police officers and four indigenous peoples (Isla 2010, 57). A couple of days after this event, the Peruvian Ombudsman Office (Defensoría del Pueblo) questioned the constitutionality of DL 1015 and DL 1073. Finally, on the eleventh day of protests, the Peruvian Congress agreed to repeal these two legislative decrees. The Congress also created a multiparty commission to review the rest of the laws AIDESEP claimed infringed upon indigenous rights (Lombardi 2010, 154).

Paralleling this multiparty commission, the García government formed a bargaining roundtable (mesa de diálogo) to dialogue with the indigenous peoples. Both AIDESEP and CONAP (Confederación de Nacionalidades Amazónicas del Perú; the Confederation of Amazonian Nationalities of Peru) were invited to this roundtable. Formed in 1987, CONAP represents twenty-five federations—fewer than half the number represented by AIDESEP. However, leaders of AIDESEP stated that as long as CONAP was in on the roundtable, they would not participate in discussions (Moyano, Ramos, and Cruz 2010, 70). Their objection had to do with CONAP's prior partaking in a contract with the state-owned oil investment company PeruPetro (Meléndez and León 2010, 463). The García government moved forward with the creation of the roundtable, with CONAP the only organization representing the indigenous people. By doing so, the government failed to understand that the root of the conflict was the debate over the legislative decrees and that it was AIDESEP, not CONAP, that had led the protests (Moyano, Ramos, and Cruz 2010, 71). These discussions did not result in effective dialogue or change in the government's policy agenda. As described in the previous chapters, the government's response was largely passive, expecting perhaps that the mobilization would die down as a consequence of protest fatigue.

Writing about Bagua and explaining how the government dealt with the Amazonian indigenous people, Reymundo and Nájar (2011, 88) invoke a recent opinion piece written by Peruvian Nobel laureate Mario Vargas Llosa in El País. The piece explains a widespread practice in Peru known as "the art of rocking" ("el arte de mecer"). In the words of Vargas Llosa:

"Rocking" (*mecer* in Spanish) is a Peruvianism that refers to the maintenance of a person in a state of uncertainty over a long period through deceit, but not by crude or common means so much as kindly and even affectionate ones. Lulling to sleep, plunging into a vague confusion, sugaring the pill, telling the tale, stunning and stupefying so that that one believes "yes" even when it's "no," and ends up wearied, abandoning and giving up whatever it was they were complaining about or had hoped to fulfill. The victim, if "rocked" with talent, in spite of realizing in a given moment that they've been lied through the teeth to, won't get annoyed, ends up resigning himself to his fate and will even become content, recognizing and admiring the good work that's been accomplished on his behalf. . . . The practical result of living one's life rocking or being rocked is that everything is delayed, goes badly, nothing works, and confusion and frustration reign everywhere.[13]

It is "a widespread practice in Peru, a national sport," the novelist adds. Reymundo and Nájar (2011) suggest that President García "rocked" Amazonian indigenous people. This so-called art of rocking could also easily be extended to other mobilizations in Peru, including Mount Quilish (chapter 5). In Quilish, representatives of the MEM "rocked" the local population who opposed Yanacocha, making them believe that a solution was attainable when, in fact, it was not.

In January 2009, the multiparty commission in charge of reviewing the decrees submitted its report to the president of the Congress, recommending the repeal of several other legislative decrees, such as DLs 1020, 1064, 1080, 1081, 1089, and in particular 1090 (the Forest and Wildlife Law). However, the Peruvian Congress—still dominated by the alliance between García's APRA and Fujimori's AF—continually postponed the discussion of the report (Moyano et al. 2010, 64). In April, Congress still had not scheduled a debate for the legislative decrees in question, and on April 9, AIDESEP began their second series of strikes, the so-called Paro Amazónico.

For more than eight weeks, thousands of Amazonian indigenous peoples blocked roads and rivers across eastern Peru. The protests went from the southeast regions of Madre de Dios and Puno, to the northeast regions of Amazonas and Loreto, and even to the central jungle districts of Junín and Huánuco (Meléndez and León 2010, 464). On April 23, around 250 indigenous protestors gathered outside Station 6 of the oil pipeline of the state-owned refinery PetroPerú located in Bagua and forced workers to shut off the oil pump (Isla 2010, 69). The pipeline, which pumps nearly forty thousand barrels of oil per day, disrupted an important energy source for coastal cities.[14] PetroPerú solicited police backup from the government and asked the Peruvian Ombudsman Office to come up with a solution to AIDESEP's petitions so that the pipeline could return to normal operations (Isla 2010, 73).

TABLE 8. The contentious legislative decrees and laws

Law 840	It expands concessions to almost 100,000 acres for use over forty years. Among other things, it facilitates the use of public waters by private irrigation projects, lowers the restrictions for the introduction of transgenic seeds, eases government control over protected areas, and establishes forest zones that could be deemed in "permanent production." The law is popularly known as the Law of the Jungle. García used the powers stated in this law in order to issue decrees 1015 and 1073.
Decrees 1015 and 1073	They overturn the internal procedures for indigenous communities to uphold the integrity of communally held territories.
Decree 1020	It provides incentives for the consolidation of rural property in exchange for agricultural loans. It transforms communal land into private property.
Decree 1064	It allows companies with concessions to get changes in zoning permits directly from Peru's central government. It eliminates prior consultation by local communities.
Decree 1080	It modifies the General Seed Law of 2000, privatizing the commercialization of seeds.
Decree 1081	It creates a national agency for the management of water resources. It redirects water access from indigenous communities to large agribusinesses.
Decree 1089	It allows for the private economic use of communal land, breaking apart traditional communal lands.
Decree 1090	It decreases the size of Peru's Forestry Heritage protection system and outlines a broad plan for how to regulate investment in the Amazon. The law frees up some 111 million acres (45 million hectares), or roughly 60 percent of Peru's jungles, for development. It is also known as the Forest and Wildlife Law (Ley Forestal y de Fauna Silvestre).

More than a month after the strike began, on May 15, AIDESEP leader Alberto Pizango Chota declared that the Amazonians were in "insurgency" (*insurgencia*) and that they "did not recognize" (*desconocieron*) the government, until action was taken regarding the decree measures (Meléndez and León 2010, 464). The following day, May 16, President García stated that "the jungle belonged to all Peruvians, and not just one group" (Reymundo and Nájar 2011, 83). Later the government charged Alberto Pizango with "rebellion, sedition and conspiracy against the state and the constitutional order," as well as with "apology of crimes against public order." Minister of Justice Rosario Fernández went further, stating that the government "will continue to prosecute the case until a guilty verdict was reached for Alberto Pizango" (quoted in Meléndez and León 2010, 464).

The president of the Congress, Javier Velásquez Quesquén (APRA), was set to debate the repeal of DL 1090 on June 4; however, the debate was blocked by Mauricio Mulder, also a member of García's APRA. In response, AIDESEP called for a national mobilization set for June 11 (Meléndez and León 2010, 464). This mobilization would never take place, as President García and his cabinet ordered 650 armed police to clear a stretch of the Fernando Belaúnde Terry highway (near Bagua) where hundreds of protestors had been blockading the important transit route. The stretch, called the Devil's Curve (La Curva del Dia blo), connects the jungle with the northern coast. According to Carmen Vildoso Chirinos, minister of women's affairs and social development, President García had "indicated to the Minister of the Interior [Mercedes Cabanillas] that it was time to finally put order in Bagua" (Lombardi 2010, 191).

The operation began in the early morning of June 5, 2009, with the goal of removing some fifteen hundred Awajún and Wampis protestors from Devil's Curve. More than four hundred police officers were dispatched to participate in the operation. At approximately 5 a.m., the first squadron of fifty-eight special operations police officers, armed with fifty-one assault rifles, five shotguns, and five tear gas launchers, approached Devil's Curve with the intent to surprise the indigenous demonstrators. A few indigenous protestors keeping watch saw the police officers and set off flares to alert the others, and within minutes, chaos erupted. Police began firing tear gas, and the indigenous peoples used pyrotechnic rockets and hunting rifles to retaliate. The indigenous peoples began burning weeds, hoping the smoke would reduce visibility for the police, and then seized some of the police's weapons to use against them. For the next few hours the conflict raged on, and police helicopters dropped tear gas bombs from the sky. Around 10:15

a.m., the police took control of the area, and the indigenous protestors began retreating into the city of Bagua.[15]

Station 6 of PetroPerú continued to be blockaded for weeks by protestors. As radio reports from Peru's leading radio station, RPP (Radio Programas del Perú), began streaming in, the more than two thousand indigenous protestors near Station 6 decided to take action. Believing the same "massacre" that was occurring at Devil's Curve would take place at Station 6, the indigenous peoples entered the facility and took thirty-eight policemen hostage. The police endured beatings throughout the morning, but in the afternoon the mob actions escalated. With spears in hand and painted faces, a group of indigenous peoples took eighteen police officers into the jungle bushes, executing twelve, while six managed to escape.

According to the Peruvian Office of the Ombudsman, thirty-three people died during the June 5 mobilization: twenty-three police officers, five indigenous peoples, and five Bagua residents, along with one missing police officer. The violence also left two hundred people injured (eighty-two with bullet injuries) and eighty-three arrested (Defensoría del Pueblo 2009). In the days following the conflict, Alberto Pizango fled to the Nicaraguan Embassy in Lima. On June 16, Pizango was granted political asylum and, shortly thereafter, traveled to Nicaragua. He would not return to Peru until a year after the conflict, when the charges against him were dropped.

Seeking to defend the government's actions, President García initially blamed the protestors for the violence. He also accused some NGOs, the Catholic Church, and even foreign agents of contributing to the protest (Lombardi 2010, 209).[16] The government also sought to portray protestors as criminals. For instance, the police chief of the Amazonas region, Victor Castañeda, believed the protestors' interests were to protect drug traffickers, who were feeding resurgent factions of the Shining Path. Former prime minister Jorge del Castillo stated that he believed the uprising was part of a "plot" led by Nationalist Party presidential candidate Ollanta Humala to overthrow the government. Others blamed Pizango and the other leaders of AIDESEP for "manipulating" the indigenous peoples (Moyano et al. 2010, 72, 78).

The campaign criminalizing protestors did not last long, however, as many around the country (including former president Alejandro Toledo) forcefully criticized the García government. Some international media outlets were calling the events "genocide." In the days following the June 5 violence, a number of international organizations put out statements denouncing the violence and defending the indigenous peoples' petitions to repeal the legislative decrees. These organizations included Amazon Watch, Amnesty International, the Council on Hemispheric Affairs, Oxfam, and the Rainforest Alliance, among others. The National Coordinator for Human Rights in Peru (Coordinadora Nacional de Derechos Humanos, CNDDHH) and dozens of its regional partners throughout the country supported AIDESEP and the overturn of the legislative decrees. At the same time, they called for peace. The government's initial response then shifted; now the Baguazo became an unfortunate event, and all of Peruvian society should share in the guilt.

On June 10, the Peruvian Congress decided to suspend the contentious legislative decrees "for an indefinite amount of time" (Meléndez and León 2010, 465). On June 17, President García called for peace and reconciliation and recognized the mistake the government had made during the conflict, primarily by not consulting with the indigenous communities about the legislative decrees before they were enacted. However, he maintained that the decrees had been issued with "good intentions" but had been "distorted" by violent groups (Meléndez and León 2010, 466). On June 19, LD 1090 and 1064 were formally repealed by Congress.

The Aftermath of Bagua

The Baguazo led to a major cabinet shakeup. On June 8, Minister of Women's Affairs and Social Development Carmen Vildoso Chirinos broke ranks with the government and quit her position in protest of its handling of the events. Including Vildoso, ten out of seventeen members of President García's cabinet were replaced in the month following the incidents in Bagua, starting with Prime Minister Yehude Simon (Lombardi 2010, 211; Meléndez and León 2010, 477). The president's approval ratings fell to historic lows: 21 percent in the month of June 2009 (Ipsos Apoyo 2009). It was the worst political crisis of his whole administration.

In the months following the conflict, rumors were still circulating that the body count was much larger than newspapers were reporting and that the government had deliberately engaged in brutal and repressive acts to forcefully end the blockade of major highways. National and international groups demanded an investigation into the details of the episode, hoping to uncover mistreatment by the executive and find a peaceful resolution to the protests.

The Peruvian Congress created an investigative commission to examine the Bagua incidents. The investigatory commission was presided over by congressional representative Guido Lombardi (Unidad Nacional). However, rather than presenting a single "official" report on Bagua, the commission broke apart and produced four "official" reports: a majority report written by Martha Moyano (Alianza para el Futuro), Eduardo Espinoza (UPP), and Juan Perry (Restauración Nacional-Alianza Nacional) (Moyano et al. 2010); and three in the minority, one by Guido Lombardi (Unidad Nacional) (Lombardi 2010), a second one by Víctor Isla (Partido Nacionalista) (Isla 2010), and the third by Luis Falla and Wilder Calderón (APRA) (Falla and Calderón 2010). These reports were released in May 2010. The inability to produce a single "official" report captures well the fragmentation of political parties documented in earlier chapters. More important, the different reports helped to divert the blame away from what many believe to be the true culprit: APRA itself. The majority report, for instance, accused "foreign elements" of inciting violence in Bagua, though it did not provide evidence to support this claim. Based on this report, the political responsibility for the Bagua events rested on Minister of the Interior Mercedes Cabanillas, Minister for External Commerce Mercedes Aráoz, and Prime Minister Yehude Simon. President García was exempted. The minority report by Isla, in contrast, recommended criminal charges involving involuntary manslaughter for the head of the National Police, Minister of the Interior Cabanillas, and President García. It also recommended charges involving false statements for Minister for External Commerce Aráoz because she had exaggerated the consequences of repealing those decrees for the US-Peru FTA.

Paralleling the four congressional reports, and that of the Defensoría del Pueblo cited earlier, in October 2009, a number of organizations came together to produce a publication entitled Perú: Alternative Report 2009 on the Fulfillment of the ILO Convention No. 169. This was an "alternative" report because it paralleled the official report from the government about its compliance with C169, which is due every five years to the ILO. The "alternative" report given to the ILO denounced the government's violations of the rights recognized in C169. The organizations involved in the elaboration of this "alternative" report included AIDESEP, CONACAMI, CCP (Confederación Campesina del Perú; the Peasant Confederation of Peru), CAN (Confederación Nacional Agraria; the National Agrarian Confederation), Asociación Paz y Esperanza, APRODEH (Asociación Pro Derechos Humanos; the Association for Human Rights), CAAAP (Centro Amazónico de Antropología y Aplicación Práctica; the Amazon Center of Anthropology and Practical Application), CARE-Perú, CNDDHH, DAR (Derecho, Ambiente y Recursos Naturales; Law, Environment, and Natural Resources), IBC (Instituto del Bien Común; the Common Good Institute), Oxfam América, and SERVINDI (Servicio en Comunicación Intercultural; Intercultural Communication Services). Overall, these reports made the case for the government to give C169 a second look.

Convention 169

The review of ILO C169, an agreement that up until then had been more symbolic than substantive, was the most important consequence of the mobilizations in Bagua. While the congressional reports failed to provide "the official story" of the Baguazo, the Lombardi report, in particular, acknowledged AIDESEP's calls for prior consultation rights as recognized in C169. The implementation of consultation rights began at the end of the García government and extended into the first years of the current government of President Ollanta Humala.

Specifically, in May 2010, while President García was still in office, the Peruvian Congress enacted the Law of Prior Consultation. The law's purpose was to match national laws with the conditions outlined in C169, which stipulated that indigenous populations were to be consulted on issues relating to their land. Shortly thereafter, AIDESEP and CONAP wrote in a statement that "[the law] requires . . . a strong commitment by the state to guarantee the implementation of this law and to ensure the inclusion of our people in national development."[17] Other national and international human rights organizations applauded the measure, including the Peruvian Ombudsman Office, the ILO, and the Office of the United Nations High Commissioner for Human Rights through James Anaya, the UN special rapporteur on the rights of indigenous people.

Predictably, President García observed the law and refused to sign it. In his view, the law was too broad and appeared to give indigenous people veto power to block any potential extraction project they opposed. García stated that the law should explicitly outline that prior consultation does not limit, suspend, or prohibit the state from adopting decisions that are in the nation's interest as a whole. In the end, the Law of Prior Consultation failed to be implemented during the García government.

In August 2011, a month after being sworn into office, President Ollanta Humala signed the law into effect. The signing ceremony took place in Bagua. In a speech, President Humala stated that the Law of Prior Consultation was an "important step" in building a nation that respects all of its communities, giving indigenous people the right to speak freely "without being subdued by economic powers" ("sin dejarse avasallar por los poderes económicos"). The events of June 5 in Bagua, though unfortunate due to the loss of human life, strengthened democracy in Peru by pushing for social inclusion as well as popular consultation mechanisms. As of this writing, the implementation of these consultation rights remains difficult, yet the substantive gains for aggrieved groups that came about as a consequence of the Baguazo are clear.

In the mobilizations of Tambogrande and Mount Quilish, the agricultural economy provided a floor of preexisting organizations, such as producers' associations (asociaciones de productores) and water users' boards (junta de usuarios de riego), through which larger defense fronts were created to oppose a specific mining company. Mining competed with agriculture in Tambogrande and Mount Quilish and presented the locals with a choice between water and mining (see chapter 1, table 1). In Bagua, in contrast, aggrieved groups drew upon their cultural identity and well-established organizations representing indigenous rights—such as AIDESEP—to fight the state. Competition between (future) extraction and agriculture was low to nonexistent in the Amazon region. Rather, the indigenous communities living there opposed exploration and extraction based on the cultural significance of the land and following their collective claims to land ownership.

In previous chapters, I have argued that the success of opposition movements against extraction hinges on their organizational strength as well as effective framing processes. Concerning the former, AIDESEP was part of a larger transnational network of organizations advocating indigenous rights—COICA. Thus, associational power and collective power in Bagua were both strong even prior to the passage of García's contentious decrees. AIDESEP's ability to call for a Paro Amazónico affecting several regions in the country speaks directly to their organizational and coalitional capacity, which was vastly underestimated (or perhaps unknown) by the García government. And with regard to the latter, framing was arguably less visible compared to the previous two cases partly because land and indigenous identity were already strongly linked to each other and partly because the Bagua events unfolded very quickly (between 2008 and 2009). In the other two cases, movement leaders actively constructed "memes" (e.g., "save the ceviche," "water is more precious than gold") in opposition to mining, and the mobilizations also unfolded over several years.

Earlier I show that political competition generally fails to promote government responsiveness due to the presence of weak parties, particularly at the subnational level (chapter 3). The Bagua events provide an opportunity to revisit some of the arguments concerning government responsiveness. On the one hand, Bagua suggests more clearly how localized protests propel government responsiveness (e.g., the implementation of C169), though the changes advocated by AIDESEP only materialized after a new government was set in place (i.e., the change from García to Humala). On the other hand, Bagua also shows that party institutions represented in the national legislature were central to the outcome of the mobilization insofar as they formulated the repeal of the decrees, though ultimately the source of responsiveness was the actions and claims of AIDESEP. Thus, while parties in Peru remain fluid and fragmented entities and are very ineffective in preventing the rise of mobilizations, they still have a role in mediating social conflicts. Altogether, as many observers agree, the Bagua events strengthened democracy in Peru by pushing for social inclusion, particularly among the indigenous population. As the conclusion shows, social inclusion improved noticeably under Humala.

CONCLUSION

THE CONSEQUENCES OF
MOBILIZATIONS

In contrast to a grievance-centered approach that privileges economic conditions over other explanatory factors, and following contributions from political process theory (Tarrow 1998; Tilly and Tarrow 2006), this book redirects attention to political conditions as central to antimarket mobilizations. These political conditions help us understand the national and subnational dynamics of protest movements across geography and time, as well as the impact of these movements on their environments. At the cross-national level, it emphasizes the moderating role of democracy in shaping societal responses to economic liberalization. It explains how economic liberalization in the context of democracy contributes to what I call the "repoliticization" of political activity (Arce 2008), showing how in some cases popular subjects adapted to market reforms and how in other cases new actors and forms of collective activity emerged in response to economic liberalization (chapter 1). These findings contradict previous literature, which anticipated the peaceful coexistence of free markets and democracy and altogether failed to explain how the combination of economic liberalization and democracy would lead to increasing levels of protest. Such literature portrays civil society as passive or incapable of organized resistance; yet protest events in the region suggest otherwise. Overall, this research emphasizes the political context in which a protest movement operates; this context, rather than the grievances or the economic threats associated with economic liberalization, better explains variations in the dynamics of protest movements.

At the subnational level, this book underscores another formal dimension of political opportunities as well as a central attribute of democracy—political competition—to untangle how and why democracy affects protest activity. In brief, political competition has long been thought to encourage government responsiveness. Extending this idea to mobilizations, political competition induces greater policy responsiveness among elected officials, such that when elected officials face significant electoral challenges, they are more likely to enact policies that can potentially reduce protest activity. However, my book shows that the effects of political competition on subnational protest vary according to the institutional setting where competition takes place (chapter 3). For instance, political competition reduces protest activity in a country like Argentina, where political parties, such as the Peronists, are relatively well established and maintain deep roots in society (Arce and Mangonnet 2013). These well-built linkages with society also allow Peronists to co-opt and demobilize popular sectors when they hold office yet encourage mass mobilizations when they are in opposition. In contrast, in a country like Peru, where political parties are weak and deeply fragmented entities, political competition generates a very different outcome. Specifically, the fragmentation of parties in Peru impairs the mechanisms of responsiveness that are typically associated with political competition and creates incentives for the use of confrontational, disruptive strategies to influence those who govern. Thus, while subnational elections are highly competitive, competition does not enhance government or policy responsiveness; rather, it is associated with higher levels of subnational political protest (chapter 3).

Whereas the first half of this book is sensitive to the variation of protest across and within countries to shed light on the factors that have led to the revival of contentious activity in Latin America in general (chapter 1) and Peru in particular (chapters 2 and 3), the second half examines the consequences of mobilizations on national outcomes. In particular, the comparative cases presented in chapters 4, 5, and 6 push political process theory toward increased interactivity, showing that in the presence of favorable political conditions (political opportunities), as in the context of democracy, societal actors can build a master frame linking resource extraction and injustices (framing processes), which in turn allows for the building of broad coalitions with diverse sets of actors (resource mobilization). This interactive approach helps us understand the conditions under which protest movements, which initially appear to be localized, segmented outbursts, are likely to produce substantive gains for aggrieved groups.

The experience of Yanacocha, for instance, stimulated a larger discussion in support of a decentralized distribution of mining rents (chapter 5). Both Tambogrande (chapter 4) and Bagua (chapter 6) legitimized the right to say "no" to further extraction, albeit for different reasons. In Tambogrande (and by extension Mount Quilish), mining competed with agriculture for water. In Bagua, extraction competed with indigenous rights and ancestral claims over native lands. The emergence of the right to prior consultation in the national agenda illustrates well the impact of these movements on their environment. By extending these rights, indigenous people, in particular, have to be consulted by the state over investment projects in their territories that are likely to affect their living conditions and cultural survival.

A couple of additional observations can be made from these case studies. First, a casual reading of these mobilizations could place the disputes over water or land as the focal point of these protests. While there is no denying that the claims over water or land did embolden aggrieved groups to mobilize, it is also true that the political environment in the post-Fujimori period was simply more favorable to mobilization. Relatedly, violence—whether it originated from the government against protestors or from aggrieved groups against mining companies—was closely watched and recorded by an emerging livelier and freer press. Democracy thus became an opportunity for mobilization and was central to the success of various antimining campaigns. Second, the protest movements represented in chapters 4, 5, and 6 also allow us to reconsider the relationship between the presence of points of access to shape policies and the surge in mobilizations. Specifically, the absence of points of access to influence policy is often seen as a motivation for protest. However, in all of these cases there were plenty of institutions, both formal (e.g., the judiciary, political parties) and informal (e.g., bargaining roundtables), involved throughout the disputes. Yet these institutions did not generate politically binding commitments. Therefore, rather than suggesting that the presence of points of access invites assimilative strategies as protest movements work with established political institutions, or that their absence encourages confrontational, disruptive strategies outside established institutionalized channels, it is more useful to think in terms of the quality of these points of access in settling these disputes. In many new democracies, like Peru, the quality of these institutions is very poor.

In this conclusion, I extend the framework presented in chapter 2 to other cases of mobilization in Peru and in other countries. The choice between mining and water summarizes well the bulk of these mobilizations. Thereafter, I examine the continuities and changes with regard to foreign investment patterns in the mining sector. Specifically, Chinese companies have emerged as a major foreign investor in Peru, and there is substantial variation in the social performance of mining companies around the country. In the final section, I return to the discussion of mining rents and their effects on national politics with an emphasis on the second García presidency, given the extraordinary rise in commodity prices at the end of the first decade of the 2000s.

Comparative Cases

The tension between agriculture and mining, and its effects on contentious episodes, is hardly unique to Tambogrande (chapter 4) or Mount Quilish (chapter 5). In fact, other cases of mobilizations support the general argument that competition with agriculture (because of limited water resources) is at the epicenter of several protests in Peru and elsewhere in the region. In addition, like Tambogrande in 2001, some of these mobilizations resulted in calls for popular referenda to stop mining activities.

Two other antimining mobilizations in Peru have invoked (and executed) consultation rights: the Tía María project of the Southern Copper Corporation (SCC) in the southern region of Arequipa and the Minera Majaz project of Monterrico Metals (UK) in the northern region of Piura. Tía María is an open-pit mine project to extract copper. The local population of the district of Cocachara in the province of Islay opposes Tía María due to its effects on farming and the water that irrigates the Valle del Tambo. In late 2009, a popular referendum rejected the mine, but similar to the Tambogrande case, neither the government nor the SCC recognized the legitimacy of the outcome of the referendum. The SCC then continued with its exploration plan by conducting an EIA. This action led to three different strikes and road-blocks in April 2010, November 2010, and March 2011. Four *comuner-os* died in the last strike when protestors clashed with the police. The Tambo Valley Defense Front (Frente de Defensa del Valle del Tambo, FDVT), which coalesced in opposition to the SCC, organized these strikes. In early 2011, the MEM requested a review of company's EIA by UNOPS (Oficina de las Naciones Unidas de Servicios para Proyectos; the United Nations Office for Project Services). UNOPS found 130 observations. The UNOPS report also made clear the lack of dialogue among the mining company, the local population in Islay, and the political authorities representing the central government (Monge, Viale, and Bedoya 2011, 321–22). As a consequence of these mobilizations, the Tía María project has been shelved for now.

The case of Minera Majaz involved the local populations of the provinces of Huancabamba and Ayabaca in the northern region of Piura. The locals sought to protect the hydrologic basins of the region against the possible extraction of copper and other minerals. They also denounced the improper transfer of communal lands to Montericco Metals (Remy 2010, 305–6). These mobilizations began in 2004 under the Toledo presidency and continued throughout the García government. Violent clashes between the police and local farmers resulted in two deaths and several cases of injury and arrests. In late 2007, organized by the mayors of three different districts (Ayavaca, Carmen de la Frontera, and Pacaipampa), a popular referendum rejected the mine. Several authors who followed the referendum point out the high level of turnout across these three districts (with 94.3 percent of voters rejecting the mine) and the presence of national and international observers—a first in popular referenda of this type. The Majaz project has been discontinued, but mining interests remain in the area (M. García 2010).

In both the Tía María and the Majaz projects, and paralleling the Tambogrande case (chapter 4), street protests, often violent, intertwined with peaceful referenda. The call for referenda, which was supported by politicians representing the local towns, appeared to indicate the exhaustion of venues or channels to stop mining. But as explained earlier, the relationship between protest and the lack of regular access to institutions is not as straightforward as it appears. There were several institutions involved across the Tía María and Majaz mobilizations, but these were simply ineffective in resolving these disputes. The quality of institutions, not the quantity, appears to matter most in explaining protest dynamics. The fact that the outcomes of the referenda were not binding also speaks volumes about the weakness of the Peruvian state, in particular the rule of law. Inasmuch as mining companies and the MEM pay no heed to the outcome of the referenda, the local population disregarded the mining concessions made by the MEM and the mining rights claimed by mining companies. The absence of the rule of law thus cut both ways.

Beyond Peru, in the small town of Famatina, located in the northwestern province of La Rioja, Argentina, aggrieved groups fought mining in the streets. In August 2011, Osisko Mining Corporation, a Canadian mining company, in partnership with state-owned Argentine company EMSE, was granted an exploratory contract to extract mostly gold and silver, along with other minerals. The governor of Rioja, Luis Beder Herrera, extended the contract to begin mining in the area.[1] However, mining interests clashed with the local agricultural economy. In particular, La Rioja's walnut and carob tree plantations provide the largest share of economic output in the area, and the mine, with its heavy reliance on water, threatened the supplies for the crucial crops of the region.[2] On January 27, 2012, approximately eleven thousand demonstrators took to the streets to block access to the mine, demanding that the governor offer up his resignation. Protestors were met with strong police repression. Although their demand for his resignation was not met, the governor did declare that the mining operations would stop until safety concerns had been addressed.[3]

There were several problems with the mining concession. For instance, the agreement between Osisko and EMSE was never made public. No environmental studies were conducted. In addition, the government made no attempt to include the public through hearings. Héctor Artuso, one of the opposition's leaders, stated: "We're not environmental or anti-mining activists. We're just regular people who reject this foreign-led model of natural resource extraction, which uses cyanide and large volumes of water."[4] To be clear, this was not the first attempt by a company to explore in the Famatina region. In 2006, protestors stopped Barrick Gold Corporation (Canada), as well as a Chinese venture company. These attempts to stop resource extraction in the region demonstrate the strong opposition to mining on environmental grounds, similar to that of Tambogrande or Cerro Quilish.

Similar to the Bagua case (chapter 6), prior consultation rights have also surfaced in Guatemala. The Marlin mine in western Guatemala, owned by Canada's Goldcorp, began operations in 2005. However, local opposition and distrust of the mine have continued to grow in the two municipalities it affects: San Miguel Ixtahuacán and Sipacapa. These municipalities have large indigenous populations, approximately 95 percent and 70 percent, respectively.[5] Unlike in Peru, however, prior consultation rights, as outlined in the International Labor Organization (ILO) Convention 169, were already a part of Guatemala's constitution. But their implementation has been very difficult, perhaps reflecting the asymmetries between Goldcorp, the largest gold-producing company in the world, and indigenous populations in Guatemala.

Denouncements by the ILO were not enough to influence Guatemalan president Alvaro Colom's decision to continue operations in the region. However, this situation changed once the opposition campaign garnered further international attention. In 2010, the UN special rapporteur on the rights of indigenous people, James Anaya, was assigned to investigate complaints into President Colom's concession practices. Following his preliminary investigation, Anaya urged the mine to suspend operations pending further investigation into human rights and environmental abuses. The fact that it took about five years for the indigenous peoples' complaints to be heard highlights the larger issue of indigenous marginalization that has continued in the twenty-first century, despite the fact that indigenous peoples make up such a large proportion of the population. Out of 137 mining concessions given, only forty-three popular consultations have been held—and all that were held yielded overwhelmingly negative votes toward mining. The mobilizations surrounding the Marlin mine approximate the Bagua case (chapter 6) insofar as protestors drew upon their cultural identity to mount a resistance campaign, rather than base organizations tied to the agriculture economy per se.

Enter the Dragon

By dismantling the statist policies of the 1970s, the economic liberalization policies of the Fujimori regime reopened foreign investment in the mining sector. The arrival of Yanacocha in 1992 and the creation of other so-called mega extractive projects (megaproyectos mineros) are widely seen as the beginnings of "new mining" in the country. These mining projects provide a lens allowing us to discuss continuities and changes with regard to foreign investment patterns in extractive industries, as well as the relationship between mining companies and society more generally.

First, in terms of investment patterns in the mining sector, the open foreign investment policies that began with Fujimori and expanded under the governments of Toledo and García reasserted the long-standing presence of foreign companies in the country. As noted in chapter 3, the beginnings of large-scale mining started in the central highlands of Peru with the arrival of Cerro de Pasco Corporation (CPC) in 1902. CPC (also known as La Compañía), along with the Southern Peruvian Copper Corporation and the Marcona Mining Corporation, represented what was then known as Gran Minería (Kruijt and Vellinga 1979).[6] These American corporations steered the Peruvian mining industry for most of the twentieth century and portrayed well the expansion of foreign capital into mining. They gradually displaced local (Peruvian) capital in extractive activities (Thorp and Bertram 1978).[7]

But the presence of Chinese investment in extractive industries represents a notable difference with regard to foreign investment patterns in Peruvian mining. In 1992, in fact, Hierro Perú (formerly the Marcona Mining Corporation) became the first state-owned company to be privatized. It was sold to China's state-run steel maker Shougang Group. The purchase price was US $120 million.[8] Today, China is the third-largest investor in the Latin American region, and over 90 percent of Chinese investment in the region is going to mineral extraction. China has also surpassed the United States as the main destination of Peru's exports. Considering the importance of Peruvian minerals, primarily copper, to the growth of the Chinese economy, Peru and China signed a free trade agreement in early 2009.

Second, there is substantial variation in the social performance of mining companies. Some companies, like Antamina, in the region of Ancash, have developed a good reputation locally and nationally and continue to do well.[9] Antamina, for instance, offers the highest wages in the industry at all levels and has also undertaken substantial corporate social responsibility efforts. It is often referred to as setting the standard that other mining companies should follow (Kotschwar, Moran, and Muir 2012). Acknowledging the importance of advancing socially responsible mining operations, David Splett, Antamina's vice president for finance, stated that "companies can fulfill a significant role in a country when institutional and social weaknesses exist" (quoted in Kotschwar, Moran, and Muir 2012, 20). Thorp (2012) agrees, noting that some mining companies function like a "state"—organizing public life and delivering basic social services—particularly in remote rural areas.

Other companies, like China's Shougang, are still way behind the learning curve. The list of infractions by Shougang is very long and ranges from poor labor practices, to breaches of environmental standards, and even to failure to meet contractual obligations. In terms of labor practices, Shougang pays the lowest wages in the industry, US $14 a day compared to US $33—which is the average miners' salary in Peru. Other mining complaints include outdated and unsafe equipment and poor housing conditions. With regard to the environment, the company has been fined several times for environmental infractions, one of which involved the collapse of tailings thickener that contaminated water supplies in the surrounding area. The company was also accused of dumping wastewater into the local bay. In early 2006, largely to protest continued abuses by the company, the regional government of Ica declared a state of environmental emergency.[10] Finally, in terms of contractual obligations, Shougang promised to invest US $150 million in community renovation projects. Yet it reneged on this promise, spending only US $35 million and later paying the US $14 million fine instead. In addition, Shougang has been late in tax payments to the government.

Finally, turning to the relationship between mining companies and society more generally, the bulk of mobilizations against the extraction of natural resources do not involve disputes between mine workers and mining companies. This may appear somewhat unusual, given that the origins of mine-worker activism can be traced to "old mining" (e.g., CPC was the largest private employer in the country for most of the twentieth century). Instead, the mobilizations typical of "new mining" involve local populations in opposition to mining companies and their "demands for rights" or "demands for services." By extension, the geographic segmentation of these mobilizations implies that these protest movements are no longer pitched at the national level and have left behind national-level unions, such as CGTP, FNTMMSP, or SUTEP of yesteryear. Consistent with the sharp decline in labor strikes in the wake of economic liberalization policies (see chapter 2, figure 3), union activism has been severely weakened. The decline is partly explained by the wave of privatizations that began in the 1990s. Massive layoffs affected Centromín and Hierro Perú in the early 1990s, along with hundreds of other state-owned enterprises. It is also partly explained by the effects of political violence, specifically the execution of key labor representatives.

In a recent article, and using the information from the National Truth Commission, Canessa (2011, 97) provides a detailed list of mining union leaders who were killed during the country's two-decade-long insurgency war. The authors of the killings include the Shining Path, the military, the national police, and a paramilitary group known as Comando Rodrigo Franco (CRF). Among the group of twenty-seven union leaders assassinated, sixteen came from Centromín Perú. The author (or authors) of those assassinations remains unknown in twelve of the twenty-seven deaths. Canessa (2011, 101–2) also discusses three assassinations that had an important effect on labor activism in Peru: Saúl Sandoval, FNTMMSP general secretary (February 13, 1989); Orestes Rodríguez, former minister of labor under the first government of García (September 22, 1990); and Pedro Huilca, CGTP general secretary (December 12, 1992). To date only the Rodríguez assassination has been attributed to the Shining Path. The assassination of leaders like Sandoval and Huilca was a major blow to union organizations, which were already severely weakened by the economic crisis of the 1980s. Only in recent years has FNTMMSP come back to life because of a more favorable political environment. And the level of strikes has been slowly rising.[11]

The Peruvian Left That Wasn't

As noted in chapter 2, the election of Alan García in 2006 reinforced the long-standing schism between Lima and the coast and the highlands of the country. The schism revealed the uneven benefits of economic liberalization, which appeared to have improved economic and social conditions in Lima and the coastal areas of Peru, but not those in the rest of the country, where the rural poor majority lives. Many observers noted that politically the country was ripe for a shift to the left, a process that was evolving elsewhere in the region (Cameron 2011a). This outcome, however, did not happen. The electoral promises of candidate García were, in fact, very different from the actions of President García.

During the 2006 presidential election, among other things, candidate García promised to revise the FTA with the United States; to uphold the autonomy of the regional governments created under Toledo; to promote sustained development by protecting the environment; and, more important, to reexamine the tax breaks and fiscal privileges granted to transnational corporations instituted under Fujimori and left untouched by Toledo (Rénique 2009). Toledo, in fact, was criticized for leaving the economy on "cruise control" as his government kept the same economic policies as Fujimori's (Cotler 2011, 546). After the election, however, the issue was not that President García paid lip service to his campaign promises, which is a common practice among Peru's political class, but rather that he sought to push neoliberalism even further.

The editorials published in *El Comercio* about "Dog in the Manger Syndrome" ("El Síndrome del Perro del Hortelano") are clear-cut examples of García's new discourse. President García encouraged the growth of big business (mostly foreign), but at the expense of those who in his view halted further economic expansion because of certain privileges. Specifically, native communities (*comunidades nativas*) in the highlands and in the Amazon stalled the extraction of minerals and woods, respectively, because of their ancestral claims on land ownership. Similarly, family fishermen (*pescadores artesanales*) opposed commercial fishing because the latter threatened their economic livelihood.

García also made repeated statements about the need to improve the country's investment climate—Peru won its first ever "investment-grade" rating in 2006. By earning this "investment-grade" rating, Peru was no longer considered a high-risk country with speculative or junk bonds. In addition, Peruvian debt was now "safer" to hold.[12] The upgrade to "investment-grade" functioned like a form of personal redemption for García, given the disastrous state of the economy he left behind after his first presidency in the 1980s. Yet the importance of the upgrade was arguably not well understood by opponents of García.[13]

Under the government of García, the country continued to experience a sizeable export bonanza, aided by record-high commodity prices and the growing Chinese demand for raw materials. As discussed in chapter 3, a portion of the revenues from extractive industries has devolved to the regions where the extraction takes place. The so-called canon minero remains the most important intergovernmental transfer linked to the exploitation of natural resources. García himself acknowledged that extractive industries were collecting windfall profits and that these extraordinary profits were not necessarily a consequence of new technologies or the competitiveness of extractive industries.

The tax breaks and fiscal privileges granted to transnational corporations date back to 1992, when Fujimori promulgated the Law of General Mining (Ley General de Minería). Some of these fiscal benefits include tax exemptions for reinvested profits (up to 80 percent); the anticipated depreciation of assets used during the first five years of exploration; the anticipated devolution of the general sales tax; and, last but not least, stability contracts averaging fifteen years for companies investing US $10 million or more. Monge, Viale, and Bedoya (2011) suggest that some of these benefits probably made sense in the early 1990s, when the country was still in the shadow of political violence and foreign investment sentiment was weak to nonexistent. In the post-Fujimori period, however, a review of these tax breaks and fiscal privileges was warranted.

President García did reexamine these fiscal benefits. However, rather than instituting a windfall profit tax, the government created the so-called Mining Program of Solidarity with the People (Programa Minero de Solidaridad con el Pueblo, PMSP). Under this program and following certain conditions, mining companies agree to pay up to 3.75 percent of their net utilities for five years. These funds are meant to improve the quality of life of the populations located in the areas where the extraction takes place. Critics disagree with the PMSP because it is a voluntary contribution (not a tax); only thirty-seven mining companies participate in the PMSP. In addition, it is controlled by the extractive companies themselves, not by the local governments where the extraction takes place. In a review of the PMSP, Humberto Campodónico noted that the contributions made to the program were "very small and unacceptable."[14] The PMSP is also popularly known as "obolo minero" to call attention to the trivial amounts paid under this program. *Obolo* (or obol) is often translated as a "half-penny" in English. To put it in simple terms, the PMSP boils down to corporate charity and abdicates the revenue extractive capacity of the Peruvian state.

Humala and the Promise of Social Inclusion

To the casual observer, protests in Peru during the first decade of the 2000s may still appear as sporadic, isolated events triggered by weak protest movements that may have had an effect on a specific local situation but are ultimately ineffectual at pushing national policy or increasing democratic responsiveness. Echoing this observation, Julio Cotler (2011, 551) recently noted that "social fragmentation conspires against the articulation of protest and their political purpose." However, as this book has shown, when taken in the aggregate and examined in the context of natural resources extraction, one can see that these mobilizations have brought about a number of important changes. Chief among them was the election of Ollanta Humala, who capitalized on the sentiments of aggrieved groups in opposition to extraction.

There are several examples showing how Humala has incorporated opposition demands into a wider policy agenda. Upon his election, for instance, Humala promulgated the Law of Prior Consultation. This law requires the government and companies to seek a consensus with local communities before approving legislation to allow nearby extraction. Humala also made the contribution to the PMSP mandatory, requiring all companies to pony up more funds to finance social programs. More important, to address the "social deficit" created by two decades of neoliberal policies, in particular the divide between Lima and the coastal areas and the rest of the country, Humala restructured the central bureaucracy. In late 2011, he created the Ministry of Development and Social Inclusion (Ministerio de Desarrollo e Inclusión Social, MIDIS). As many observers have pointed out, social inclusion has become a defining feature of his government.

According to Humala, the government's push for social inclusion does not threaten the expansion of extractive activities. Rather, it seeks to strike a balance between mining and the social needs of the country. "We are not anti-mining, but we have to make mining serve the whole population and not just a minority," Humala stated.[15] Of course, statements like this one make it look simpler than it is, yet very few would deny that Humala's ideas represent a welcome departure from García's "dog in the manger" vision. The impact of Humala's fresh political discourse and noticeable policy changes on mobilizations remains to be seen. So far they have not lessened mobilizations.

APPENDIX

BASE DE PROTESTAS SOCIALES DEL PERÚ

The dataset covers thirty-one years of contentious activity, from January 1980 until December 2010. It spans six different presidencies: Fernando Belaúnde (1980–85), Alan García (1985–90), Alberto Fujimori (1990–2000), Valentín Paniagua (2000–2001), Alejandro Toledo (2001–6), and Alan García (2006–11). The dataset comes from the local print media, utilizing three of the country's largest newspapers based on circulation: *El Comercio*, *El Expreso*, and *La República*. It records 17,035 protest events by date (day, month, year) and location (district, province, department, or region) across six main categories: the type of protest, the type of actor, the type of demand, the target of protest, the level of violence, and the geographic setting of the protest event (for additional information about the dataset, see Arce 2014).

Before describing these categories, a note on the advantages and disadvantages of using the print media to record protest events is warranted. Generally, newspapers tend to overreport protest events when protests are high and, conversely, to underreport protest events when protests are low. Similarly, the geographic proximity of the newspaper to the protest event tends to inflate the reporting of some protests in comparison to others. Moreover, the reporting of protest events can be slanted depending on the ideological orientation or "political culture" of the newspapers (see Barranco and Wisler 1999). Aside from these general concerns, the Fujimori period poses additional challenges for the Peruvian case. Specifically, Conaghan (2002) describes how the Fujimori regime (through Vladimiro Montesinos) utilized bribes to collude with the local print media, boasting the performance of the regime while belittling the opposition. The stifling of a free press under Fujimori may have affected the reporting of some protest events, particularly in the late 1990s (see also McMillan and Zoido 2004).

The dataset addresses some of the disadvantages of using the print media to record protest events by using newspapers with different ideological perspectives or "political cultures." For instance, *La República* emerged as a leading opposition newspaper during the Fujimori period. *El Comercio, El Expreso,* and *La República* also have national reach and predate the waves of protest documented in chapter 2. *El Comercio, El Expreso,* and *La República* were founded in 1839, 1961, and 1981, respectively. In this way, the dataset corrects the potential overreporting or underreporting of protest events as a result of geographic proximity or the waves of contentious activity themselves.

Description of Variables

Protest event: an action or claim by a group of three or more persons (hereafter collective actors) separate from the organs of the state at a given point in time against economic and/or political elites and institutions.

Type of Protest (Action)

Mobilization or march: a protest event that involves movement of collective actors through a public space—usually in some form of line.

Work stoppage: when collective actors announce a stop in working for a definite amount of time.

Strike: when workers of the public or private sector stop work for an indefinite amount of time.

Hunger strike: when collective actors fast to make a political or economic claim.

Roadblock: when collective actors obstruct the free movement of vehicles or people utilizing tires, tree branches, rocks, and other objects.

Sit-in (plantón): the physical occupation of a public or private space by collective actors making a political or economic claim.

Takeover (toma): when collective actors occupy—usually with violence—a public or private entity.

Clash (enfrentamiento): a protest event with some degree of violence involving members of the same group or different groups of actors. It does not include members of law enforcement.

Land seizure: the occupation of land by collective actors.

Others: actions other than the ones mentioned above.

Type of Actors

Students: includes schools and colleges of higher education.

Townspeople: residents of a town whose demands are related to quality of life, including demands for services, infrastructure, or care for the environment.

General public: citizens from different demographic groups gathered around a national symbol (such as the national flag).

Fronts: formally constructed (recast) associations that represent various organizations both regional and national.

Public sector: workers associated with any institution of the state, for example, teachers, doctors, retirees, and municipal workers.

Private sector: workers associated with a business or private enterprise.

Independent workers: workers relying on their own means of sustenance.

Small farmers: workers in the agricultural sector.

Political authorities: elected officials from the electoral contests organized by the National Office of Electoral Processes (ONPE).

Political parties: leaders and members of political parties.

Other actors: actors of other types that do not fit in the above categories.

Type of Demand (Claim)

Labor: demands for improvements to working conditions, such as wages.

Budget: claims related to fiscal management, subsidies, taxes, and fees.

Administrative: claims related to the performance of public sector officials, as well as the internal organization of institutions that belong to the public sector.

Political: demands that involve elected political authorities and their policies.

Social: demands for a better standard of living, for example, requesting the construction of schools, hospitals, bridges, and homes, and demands to clean up environmental pollution.

Other: other demands that do not fit in the above categories.

Target of Protest

Central government: when demands are directed at the executive.

Ministry: when demands are directed at a specific ministry of the executive.

Municipality: when demands are directed to local governments.

Regional government: when demands are directed to regional governments.

Judiciary: when demands are directed at the judiciary.

Legislature: when demands are directed at the legislative arm of government.

Private enterprise: when demands are directed at a business or private-sector institution.

Universities: when demands are directed at a public or private college or university.

JNE/ONPE: when demands are directed at the National Jury of Elections (JNE) or the National Office of Electoral Processes (ONPE).

Others: any other option that does not fit in the above categories.

Level of Violence

Low: when there has been no damage to property or injury to persons.

Medium: when there has been some damage to property.

High: when there has been some injury to persons.

Geographic Setting

Local: if the protest is limited to a town or a district.

Regional: if the protest takes place in more than one district or involves collective actors from several districts or provinces of a region.

National: if the protest occurs in and involves collective actors from several regions.

NOTES

Introduction

1. In keeping with Goodwin and Jasper's (2003, 3) definition, this book uses the term "political" or "social protest" to refer to "the act of challenging, resisting, or making demands upon authorities, powerholders, and/or cultural beliefs and practices by some individual or group." The term "protest" or "protest movement" refers to organized and sustained challenges.

2. The terms "organizational capacity" and "coalitional capacity" are taken from Silva (2009, chapter 2). Chapter 1 draws on these terms to understand the relative strength of aggrieved groups opposed to extraction vis-à-vis those in support of mining.

3. As Peru's former minister of energy and mining Juan Valdivia put it, "the mining agenda is the agenda of national development" (quoted in Arellano-Yanguas 2008, 9). Similarly, Carlos Herrera, President Humala's minister of energy and mining, stated: "The success of Peru depends on mining" (*El Comercio*, Nov. 21, 2011).

4. Yashar (1998) explains the importance of systemwide or macro political opportunities advanced by political liberalization for the emergence of indigenous movements in Latin America.

5. The discussion concerning the relationship between electoral competition and government responsiveness follows Cleary 2010 (chapter 2). The notion that competition leads to fewer protests because of policy responsiveness follows Wilkinson 2004.

6. As Tarrow (1998) writes, protest "is used by people who lack regular access to institutions."

7. The terms "associational power" and "collective power" are taken from Silva 2009 (chapter 2).

8. The discussion on the subnational comparative analysis follows Snyder 2001 and Beer and Mitchell 2004.

9. Substantive gains are defined as changes of policy in response to protest.

10. The quote comes from a cable communication dated May 10, 2005, from the US Embassy in Lima, as published by WikiLeaks in *El Comercio*. For a discussion about mining conflicts, see Scurrah 2008; Bebbington 2007; and De Echave et al. 2009.

Chapter 1. Rethinking the Consequences of Economic Liberalization

1. In this book the terms "economic liberalization" and "globalization" are used interchangeably, implying policies that seek to reduce state intervention in the economy. Examples include trade liberalization, privatization of state enterprises, and domestic and international financial liberalization.

2. The preoccupation with stability and order from earlier studies follows what is known as "antistate theory," where protest is largely seen a threat to the legitimacy of democracy or the political system as a whole. Alternatively, protest could simply be another form of conventional political participation in modern democracies. Norris, Walgrave, and Van Aelst (2005) develop these theoretical perspectives for the case of postindustrial Belgium.

3. The repoliticization perspective highlights three broad patterns of popular resistance to economic liberalization across the Latin American region. First, traditional class-based actors have continued to mobilize against economic reform policies. Second, new forms of contention involving both actors and types of protests have emerged to challenge economic liberalization policies. Finally, economic liberalization has provoked a number of geographically territorialized protests that have had significant political consequences at the national level. Collectively, these responses speak of the changing nature of antigovernment mobilizations against economic liberalization in the context of democracy. The depoliticization/repoliticization debate draws heavily on Arce and Kim 2011 (255–60) and Bellinger and Arce 2011 (689–92).

4. Meyer (2004) provides a review of the literature on political opportunities. For a critique of this concept—especially concerning its expansive use—see Goodwin and Jasper 2004.

5. A meme can be a slogan, a phrase, or a symbol; it becomes a meme when it spreads from person to person. Social movement leaders seek to invent memes that will catch on with aggrieved groups.

6. To be clear, Silva (2009) also highlights other conditions that contributed to the rise of contentious activity in Latin America, such as the presence or absence of political associational space, the presence or absence of economic crisis, the application of framing and brokerage mechanisms to form coalitions among anti-neoliberal movements, and the reformist nature of major mobilizing forces excluding armed insurrection. But overall, anti-neoliberal contention had a common origin, summed up in the grievances that were generated by the neoliberal project. These grievances served "as a unified element for diverse protest groups" (Silva 2009, 266).

7. In these large-N studies, the measures of economic liberalization include Morley, Machado, and Pettinato 1999 and the KOF Index of Globalization (Dreher, Gaston, and Martens 2008). The measures of political democracy

include Polity IV (Marshall and Jaggers 2009); Freedom House; Mainwaring, Brinks, and Pérez-Liñán 2001; and Cheibub, Gandhi, and Vreeland 2010.

8. Figure 1 includes the following countries: Argentina, Bahamas, Barbados, Belize, Bolivia, Brazil, Chile, Colombia, Costa Rica, Dominican Republic, Ecuador, El Salvador, Guatemala, Guyana, Haiti, Honduras, Jamaica, Mexico, Nicaragua, Panama, Paraguay, Peru, Suriname, Trinidad and Tobago, Uruguay, and Venezuela. CNTS is the most commonly used measure of mobilizations in cross-national studies. It is compiled from a single news source, the *New York Times*. Alternatively, the High Profile Strikes Dataset (HPSD) comes from press reports and draws from a broad range of sources of information (nearly seven hundred news sources from the Nexis database) (Robertson and Teitelbaum 2011, 670). Comparing HPSD with CNTS, G. B. Robertson and Teitelbaum (2011, 670) note that "the number of events recorded for Latin America was broadly similar." For instance, CNTS records 260 strikes compared to HPSD's 280 strikes for the period 1979–2006. Similarly, the maximum number of strikes for CNTS in any given year was six, compared to five for the HPSD dataset. The similarities across these two datasets, particularly for the Latin American region, provide greater confidence concerning the repoliticization trends outlined in this chapter.

9. As one would expect, the populous province of Buenos Aires and the populous region of Lima concentrate the greatest level of mobilizations in Argentina and Peru, respectively. The information about the southern regions in Peru with the most protest is taken from the empirical analysis shown in chapter 3.

10. Kitschelt (1986) examined the dynamics of antinuclear movements in four advanced industrial democracies (France, Sweden, the United States, and West Germany). He focused on the openness of political systems to new demands (political input structures), as well as the capacity of political systems to implement policies (political output structures). In this book, I emphasize the former structures as they relate to the quality of representation as embodied in political parties.

11. As Wilkinson (2004) writes, increasing political competition in Indian politics made the minority vote gradually more important, and thus various minority groups have gained from affirmative action policies in government jobs and seats, as well as cultural protections and special economic programs.

12. Regarding protest against the extraction of mineral resources, see Scurrah 2008; Bebbington 2007; and De Echave et al. 2009, among others.

13. The terms "associational power" and "collective power" are taken from Silva 2009 (chapter 2).

Chapter 2. Waves of Contentious Politics in Peru

1. Representative works include Bravo 2009; Caballero and Cabrera 2008; Meléndez and León 2009; Pizarro, Trelles, and Toche 2004; and Tanaka and Vera 2008.

2. Fujimori's neoliberal reforms, in particular, worsened centralization

patterns because Lima provided economies of scale that could not be easily reproduced by the rest of the country (Gonzáles de Olarte 2000; Arce 2008).

3. Before Toledo's reforms, departments were considered administrative units of the central government, which appointed governors (*prefectos*) for each department. Since the early 1980s until 2002, in contrast, provincial- and district-level mayors have been chosen in municipal elections every three years.

4. Toledo had run previously for the presidency in 1995 under the party label País Posible and again in 2000 with his current party label Perú Posible.

5. "World Bank: Peru to Post Asian Growth Rate by Expanding 5.5% This Year," *Andina: Agencia Peruana de Noticias,* Oct. 10, 2013. Similarly, in 2011 *Forbes* magazine declared Peru the second-best country in Latin America in which to do business, next to Chile. See "Best Countries for Business," *Forbes Magazine,* Oct. 3, 2011.

6. The analysis of García's electoral strategy draws on Cameron 2011a.

7. See Mario Vargas Llosa, "El arte de mecer," *El País,* Feb. 21, 2010.

8. Toledo frequently used indigenous symbols and discussed issues of concern to indigenous voters during his presidential campaign. In 2000, for instance, he led a major protest in opposition to Fujimori's third presidential term, calling it *la marcha de los cuatro suyos* (the march of the four *suyos,* or the march of the four corners of the Incan empire). During a widely publicized campaign stop, Toledo's wife—Eliane Karp, who speaks fluent Quechua—invoked Incan deities known as *apus* on behalf of her husband and suggested that Toledo represented the reincarnation of the Inca Pachacuti. President Toledo subsequently inaugurated his term in a ceremony at the ruins of Machu Picchu and there signed the Declaration of Machu Picchu in support of indigenous rights. Toledo often referred to himself using the term *cholo*—which is colloquially used to describe dark-skinned individuals, including those of indigenous decent, and is still regarded as an insult by most Peruvians (M. E. García 2005, 28)—in order to draw attention to his Andean origins. On the politicization of indigenous voting, see Raymond and Arce 2013.

9. "Blood in the Jungle," *Economist,* June 13, 2009.

10. Similar to Yashar (1998, 31), I define political liberalization as "increased freedoms of association, expression, and the press."

11. The distinction between "good" and "bad" news comes from Almeida 2009.

12. Cross-national studies show that economic indicators, such as GDP per capita and GDP growth, are not good predictors of mobilizations.

13. Freedom House classifies regimes as "free," "partly free," and "not free" using the average of their civil liberties and political rights indices, which range from 1 to 7, with higher values indicating less freedom. Regimes that have an average rating 2.5 or below are considered "free," regimes with an average rating in the 3 to 5 range are considered "partly free," and regimes rated 5.5 or higher are considered "not free."

14. On average, the number of workers involved in strikes was 470,325 during the 1970s. These figures were taken from the Instituto Nacional de Estadística e Informática.

Chapter 3. Mobilization by Extraction

1. The ICMM was created in 2010 in response to the reputation problems affecting the industry as well as the confidence of investors.

2. The most recent report from the Peruvian Office of the Ombudsman (June 2012) records 247 conflicts, of which 60.7 percent (or 150) are categorized as socioenvironmental (*socioambientales*). This category of conflict deals with mobilizations as a consequence of resource extraction.

3. The distinction between mobilizations involving "demands for rights" and "demands for services" comes from Javier Torres Seoane, the news director of the Asociación de Servicios Educativos Rurales (SER). Javier Torres Seoane, personal interview with the author, Lima, Aug. 5, 2011.

4. Arellano-Yanguas (2010) notes that what I have called mobilizations involving "demands for services" became more common toward the end of the 2000s. Arellano-Yanguas's study focuses on this type of mobilization.

5. This section draws on Wibbels 2004, 205–7.

6. Across the 2001, 2006, and 2011 national elections, the effective number of legislative parties was 4.37, 3.78 and 3.97, respectively.

7. During the 2010–14 period, La Libertad is the only regional government controlled by APRA.

8. Similarly, Meléndez (2005) has observed how the absence of large-scale secondary organizations in support of regional politicians often leads these political actors to pursue political office solely for private gain. Several regional politicians, in fact, have been involved in corrupt practices (Arce 2008).

9. These twenty-five regions include Peru's twenty-four departments and the constitutional province of Callao.

10. The effective number of parties (ENP) is a commonly used indicator of political competition. However, given the fluidity and weakness of the Peruvian party system, this indicator says more about political fragmentation than competition. I thank an anonymous reviewer for bringing up this point.

11. Rather than focusing on the distribution of mineral rents, the geographical concentration of mining production is another way to illustrate the variation of subnational protests in the country. For instance, 70 percent of mining production is located in only six departments: Ancash, Arequipa, Cajamarca, La Libertad, Moquegua, and Pasco (Thorp 2012, 121). Yet the regions of Ancash (25.7 protests) and La Libertad (19.6 protests) have more protests than the sample mean of 17.6 (excluding the region of the capital city of Lima) and the regions of Cajamarca (13.7 protests), Arequipa (11.0 protests), Moquegua (9.7 protests), and Pasco (8.7 protests).

12. Steven Levitsky, "No veo una crisis política prolongada tras la elección," *La República*, June 5, 2011.

13. According to Silva (2009), aggrieved social actors in Peru failed to create the brokerage mechanisms conducive to coalitions among anti-neoliberal movements, and thus contentious activity remained geographically dispersed.

Chapter 4. Lime Wars

1. Limes and mangos contribute approximately US $147.5 million to the national economy, mostly in the form of exports. The irrigation project also provides clear benefits to the local ecosystem. Due to the groundwater produced by the irrigation project, an abundance of algarrobo trees has accumulated over time (Oxfam America 2001). These trees provide essential cover to the region, preventing expedited desertification and protecting the valley from the harsh winds and rainfall during frequent El Niño events.

2. The population of the district of Tambogrande at the time of the mobilizations against MMC was approximately sixty-eight thousand people. Tambogrande is one out of nine districts of the province of Piura.

3. As noted earlier, the agricultural economy makes available a range of preexisting organizations, such as producers' associations (*asociaciones de productores*) and water users' boards (*junta de usuarios de riego*). The organizations represented by defense front included the Junta Administrativa de Regantes del Valle de San Lorenzo, the Asociación de Colonos, and the Asociación de Agricultores de Mango y Limón, among others (Paredes 2008, 273).

4. The investigation that followed was inconclusive. In the eyes of Baca's family and friends, a satisfactory resolution to the case was never reached. He "was murdered when he and his son were going to their land property to effectuate the payment to the farmers. A shot towards his heart killed him immediately" (Olortegui 2007, 34).

5. Prior to the popular referendum, residents of Tambogrande signed a petition supporting agriculture and asking for an end to the mining project. The front collected 28,374 notarized signatures and sent them to then-president Valentín Paniagua (De Echave et al. 2009, 34).

6. The procedure allowed thirty days to present observations to the EIA. The MEM then evaluated the EIA and delivered a report, which then allowed MMC ninety days to incorporate the observations of the report into their procedure. Finally, another thirty days were given for the MEM to decide whether or not to allow MMC to continue with operations.

7. As discussed in chapter 1, the relative strength of aggrieved groups compared to those in support of mining is shaped by their associational power and collective power.

8. The Mesa Técnica included organizations such as APRODEH, CEPES, CooperAcción, ECO, FREDEPAZ, SPDA, the Asociación Civil Labor, the Comisión Episcopal de Acción Social, the Diaconía para la Justicia y la Paz de Piura, and the Coordinadora Nacional de Derechos Humanos (De Echave et al. 2009, 32).

9. Other international NGOs were the Mineral Policy Center, the Environmental Mining Council of British Columbia, and Friends of the Earth from Costa Rica and Ecuador.

10. This is particularly important in a region, such as northern Peru, that is constantly plagued by El Niño events. If not properly maintained, storage facilities can become unstable during El Niño storms and leak their contents elsewhere.

11. The 1993 census was the census conducted closest to the time of the mobilization.

Chapter 5. Mining Mountains

1. "Tangled Strands in Fight over Peru Gold Mine," *New York Times,* June 14, 2010.

2. "Tangled Strands in Fight over Peru Gold Mine."

3. "Tangled Strands in Fight over Peru Gold Mine." In a sworn deposition, Vladimiro Montesinos admitted accepting a US $4 million bribe from Newmont in order to ensure the company's victory in the 1998 Supreme Court decision. Montesinos also stated that then-US president Bill Clinton's secretary of state for Latin America and US ambassador to Peru, John Hamilton, had pressured Fujimori to ensure Newmont's victory in the case (Monning 2005).

4. Open-pit mines like Yanacocha are typically enlarged until the mineral resource is exhausted.

5. Bebbington (2007) discusses the earliest environmental issues involving water contamination in Cajamarca.

6. The narrative of these events follows Salas 2006. Salas was the leader of the defense front and wrote a detailed report on the events of Quilish.

7. It was expected that 2004 would be a very dry year in Cajamarca. The drought worked to increase the scale of contention.

8. Other prominent names include Andrés Zamora and Isaías Vasquez, who were group leaders.

9. The concept of "scale-shift" is defined as "a change in the number and level of coordinated contentious actions to a different focal point, involving a new range of actors, different objects, and broadened claims" (McAdam, Tarrow, and Tilly 2001, 331).

10. The 5 percent ownership by the International Finance Corporation (IFC) explains CAO's connection to the World Bank.

11. Some examples from Yanacocha include: the Tecnificación de la Producción del Cuy como Alternativa Rentable and the Centro de Innovación Tecnológica de Joyería (De Echave et al. 2009, 93–95).

12. Between 1992 and 2005, Yanacocha paid about US $389 million in total *canon minero,* with US $189 million going to the appropriate local institutions (Lingán 2008, 38).

Chapter 6. Blood in the Jungle

1. To be clear, the opening of the Amazon was strictly a clash between the García government and AIDESEP. Moreover, unlike the cases described in the previous chapters, the participation of local mayors or regional presidents was largely absent in the case of Bagua. Therefore, the expectation that subnational government could potentially step up to resolve these disputes was simply not there.

2. In Spanish: "Alan García ha parecido el Presidente de CONFIEP en estos cinco años."

3. "García's Booming Peru Economy May Not Help Defeat Chavez-Like Challenger," *Bloomberg News,* June 8, 2010.

4. The editorials were: "El síndrome del perro del hortelano," *El Comercio,* Lima, Oct. 28, 2007; "Receta para acabar con el perro del hortelano," *El Comercio,* Lima, Nov. 4, 2007; and "El perro del hortelano contra el pobre," *El Comercio,* Lima, Mar. 2, 2008. For further discussion of these editorials, see M. García 2011.

5. The editorials, as Levitsky (2013, 309) puts it, "compared protesters to the dog in Aesop's fable, whose snarling prevents hungry cattle from eating."

6. García's editorial "El síndrome del perro del hortelano" was translated as "The Dog in the Manger Syndrome," *Andean Air Mail & Peruvian Times,* Lima, Oct. 30, 2007. This text follows this translation with some minor, nonsubstantive changes.

7. "¿Cómo superar 'el síndrome del perro del horteano'?" *El Comercio,* Lima, Nov. 4, 2007.

8. The roots of the organization date back to the nationalist military regime of General Juan Francisco Velasco Alvarado (1969–75), with the passage of the Law of Native Communities (Ley de Comunidades Nativas). This law began the process of granting land titles on behalf of native communities.

9. AIDESEP's main objectives include representing the interests of the indigenous people of the Amazon; guaranteeing the conservation and development of the cultural identity, land, and beliefs of all the indigenous communities in the Amazon; and promoting sustainable development. According to the Organization of American States (OAS), AIDESEP has received funding from organizations such as Oxfam, Nouvelle Planette, NOVID, Bread for the World Foundation, the Norwegian Agency for Development (NORAD), and the Rain Forest Foundation.

10. "El verdadero perro del hortelano," *Lucha indígena,* June 14, 2009, 8.

11. "Peruvian Government, Amazonian Indigenous Groups Remain Deadlocked," *Environment News Service,* June 15, 2009.

12. "Indígenas se declaran en insurgencia," *La República,* May 16, 2009.

13. Mario Vargas Llosa, "El arte de mecer," *El País,* Feb. 21, 2010. Vargas Llosa's opinion piece was translated as "The Peruvian Art of Rocking," *Living in Peru,* Mar. 22, 2010. This text follows this translation with some minor, nonsubstantive changes.

14. "Blood in the Jungle," *Economist*, June 13, 2009.

15. In the cities of Bagua, Utcubamba, and Jaén episodes of violence broke out, resulting in damage to public and private property and the deaths of five citizens. Townspeople, not AIDESEP protestors, were to blame for these incidents, some acting in solidarity with the indigenous peoples and others taking advantage of the confusion to perpetrate violence (Moyano et al. 2010, 79).

16. The foreign influences were Venezuela and ALBA (Alianza Bolivariana para los Pueblos de Nuestra América).

17. "Congress Passes Indigenous' Consultation Law," *Latin American Press*, June 3, 2010.

Conclusion: The Consequences of Mobilizations

1. Luis Beder Herrera was a politician of the Frente Para la Victoria (FPV), a faction of the Partido Justicialista (PJ), or Peronist Party. In the 1980s, when he was a provincial deputy, Luis Beder Herrera proposed and sponsored a bill that made open-pit mining illegal in the province. His antimining stance changed once he became governor of La Rioja.

2. "Argentina: Water Is Worth More Than Gold," *Latin American Weekly Report*, Feb. 2, 2012, 7.

3. "Canadian Firm Osisko Halts Argentina Mining Project," *BBC News*, Jan. 31, 2012.

4. "Argentine Province Suspends Open-Pit Gold Mining Project Following Protests," *MercoPress: South Atlantic News Agency*, Jan. 31, 2012.

5. "Guatemala: Colom Pulled upon Indigenous Rights," *Latin American Weekly Report*, June 24, 2010, 13–14.

6. The Southern Peruvian Copper Corporation was created in 1952, and its operations began in the region of Tacna. In 2005, it acquired Minera Mexico and was renamed Southern Copper Corporation (SCC). The Marcona Mining Corporation was established in 1953 in the region of Ica.

7. In the 1970s, the military expropriated companies like CPC and Marcona in defense of national interests and social necessities. CPC became Centromín Peru. Marcona Mining Corporation became Hierro Perú.

8. In 1997, Doe Run bought Centromín Peru.

9. The shareholders of Compañía Minera Antamina include BHP Billiton (33.75 percent), Xstrata (33.75 percent), Teck (22.50 percent), and Mitsubishi Corporation (10.00 percent).

10. Kotschwar, Moran, and Muir (2012) note that most Chinese companies, including Shougang, are not members of the International Council on Mining and Metals (ICMM), an international organization dedicated to the sustainable development of mining operations.

11. "Mineros comienzan huelga indefinida," *La República*, Apr. 30, 2007; "Mineros convocan a huelga indefinida para fin de mes," *La República*, Sept. 19, 2013.

12. This assessment comes from credit agencies (e.g., Standard and Poor's, Moody's, and Fitch), based on a country's ability to service its own debt, among other risk factors.

13. Beyond the economy, García also sought to slow down the decentralization process. He supported a system of bilateral relations with individual regional governments, rather than the National Assembly of Regional Governments (Asamblea Nacional de Gobiernos Regionales, ANGR). Evaluating García's take on decentralization, Ballón (2011, 200) wrote: "Lima does not appear particularly interested in pushing decentralisation ahead faster, constantly pointing to the inadequacies of regional government." García also went after the work of NGOs. He accused them of promoting instability and the undue influence of foreign governments over national interests. García then redirected ACPI (Agencia Peruana de Cooperación Internacional) to fiscally audit the donations received by NGOs (Llona 2008).

14. Humberto Campodónico, "García, óbolo e impuesto a las sobreganancias mineras," *La República,* Apr. 1, 2011.

15. "Humala: Gold and Water, not Gold or Water," *Latin American Weekly Report,* Nov. 24, 2011.

REFERENCES

Agüero, Felipe, and Jeffrey Stark, eds. 1998. *Fault Lines of Democracy in Post-Transition Latin America*. Miami: North-South Center Press.

Alfaro, Santiago, Enrique Amayo, Eduardo Ballón, Felipe Bedoya, Teresa Cabrera, Luis Chirinos, Edgardo Cruzado, Jennie Dador, Mariel García, Martín Garro, Raúl Mauro, Carlos Monge, Modesto Montoya, Juan Narváez, Cosmin Olteanu, Erick Pajares, Jorge Rodríguez, Jean-Michel Servet, Vicente Sotelo, Eduardo Toche, and Claudia Viale, eds. 2011. *Perú hoy: El quinquenio perdido. Crecimiento con exclusión*. Lima: DESCO.

Almeida, Paul, and Hank Johnston. 2006. "Neoliberal Globalization and Popular Movements in Latin America." In H. Johnston and P. Almeida, eds., *Latin American Social Movements: Globalization, Democratization, and Transnational Networks*. Lanham, MD: Rowman and Littlefield. 3–18.

Almeida, Paul D. 2007. "Defensive Mobilization: Popular Movements against Economic Adjustment Policies in Latin America." *Latin American Perspectives* 34 (3): 123–39.

Almeida, Paul D. 2008. "The Sequencing of Success: Organizing Templates and Neoliberal Policy Outcomes." *Mobilization* 13 (2): 165–87.

Almeida, Paul D. 2009. "Globalization and Collective Action." In K. Leich and J. Jenkins, eds., *Handbook of Politics: State and Society in Global Perspective*. New York: Springer. 305–26.

Arce, Moisés. 2005. *Market Reform in Society: Post-Crisis Politics and Economic Change in Authoritarian Peru*. University Park: Pennsylvania State University Press.

Arce, Moisés. 2008. "The Repoliticization of Collective Action after Neoliberalism in Peru." *Latin American Politics and Society* 50 (3): 37–62.

Arce, Moisés. 2010a. "Algunos apuntes sobre los movimientos y protestas sociales en el Perú." In Carlos Meléndez and Alberto Paniagua, eds., *La iniciación de la política: El Perú en perspectiva comprada*. Lima: Fondo Editorial de la Pontificia Universidad Católica del Perú. 273–94.

Arce, Moisés. 2010b. "Parties and Social Protest in Latin America's Neoliberal Era." *Party Politics* 16 (5): 669–86.

Arce, Moisés. 2014. "Base de Protestas Sociales del Perú Dataset." Columbia: University of Missouri. http://faculty.missouri.edu/~arcem/.

Arce, Moisés, and Paul T. Bellinger. 2007. "Low-Intensity Democracy Revisited: The Effects of Economic Liberalization on Political Activity in Latin America." *World Politics* 60 (1): 97–121.

Arce, Moisés, and Wonik Kim. 2011. "Globalization and Extra-Parliamentary Politics in an Era of Democracy." *European Political Science Review* 3 (2): 253–78.

Arce, Moisés, and Jorge Mangonnet. 2013. "Competitiveness, Partisanship, and Subnational Protest in Argentina." *Comparative Political Studies* 46 (8): 895–919.

Arce, Moisés, and Roberta Rice. 2009. "Societal Protest in Post-Stabilization Bolivia." *Latin American Research Review* 44 (1): 88–101.

Arellano-Yanguas, Javier. 2008. "A Thoroughly Modern Resource Curse? The New Natural Resource Policy Agenda and the Mining Revival in Peru." Working paper, Brighton, United Kingdom: University of Sussex, Institute of Development Studies.

Arellano-Yanguas, Javier. 2010. "Local Politics, Conflict and Development in Peruvian Mining Regions." PhD dissertation, University of Sussex.

Avila, Gustavo, Claudia Viale, and Carlos Monge. 2011. "Extractive Industries and Their Imprint." In Crabtree 2011, 159–85.

Azpur, Javier, Rosa Pizarro, Luis Sirumbal, Eduardo Toche, Laura Trelles, and Cynthia Zavalla, eds. 2004. *Perú hoy: Los mil días de Toledo*. Lima: DESCO.

Ballón, Eduardo. 2011. "Decentralisation." In Crabtree 2011, 187–216.

Banaszak, Lee Ann. 1996. *Why Movements Succeed or Fail: Opportunity, Culture, and the Struggle for Woman Suffrage*. Princeton, NJ: Princeton University Press.

Banco Central de Reserva del Perú (BCRP). 2012. *Memoria 2012*. Lima: Banco Central de Reserva del Perú.

Banks, Arthur S. 2010. Cross-National Time-Series Data Archive. Databanks International. Jerusalem, Israel. http://www.databanksinternational.com.

Barranco, José, and Dominique Wisler. 1999. "Validity and Systematicity of Newspaper Data in Event Analysis." *European Sociological Review* 15 (3): 301–22.

Basadre, Jorge. 1978. *Perú: Problema y posibilidad*. Lima: Banco Internacional del Perú.

Bebbington, Anthony, ed. 2007. *Minería, movimientos sociales y respuestas campesinas: Una ecología política de transformaciones territoriales*. Lima: Instituto de Estudios Peruanos.

Bebbington, Anthony, ed. 2009. "Latin America: Contesting Extraction, Producing Geographies." *Singapore Journal of Tropical Geography* 30 (1): 7–12.

Bebbington, Anthony, M. Connarty, W. Coxshall, H. O'Shaughnessy, M. Williams. 2007. *Mining and Development in Peru, with Special Reference to the*

Rio Blanco Project, Piura. London: Peru Support Group.

Beer, Caroline, and Neil J. Mitchell. 2004. "Democracy and Human Rights in the Mexican States: Elections or Social Capital?" *International Studies Quarterly* 48 (2): 293–312.

Bellinger, Paul T., and Moisés Arce. 2011. "Protest and Democracy in Latin America's Market Era." *Political Research Quarterly* 64 (3): 688–704.

Benford, Robert D., and David A. Snow. 2000. "Framing Processes and Social Movements: An Overview and Assessment." *Annual Review of Sociology* 26: 611–39.

Boulding, Carew. 2010. "NGOs and Political Participation in Weak Democracies: Sub-National Evidence on Protest and Voter Turnout from Bolivia." *Journal of Politics* 72 (2): 456–68.

Bravo, Fernando. 2009. "El desempeño del estado y la conflictividad social." *Coyuntura: Análisis Económico y Social de Actualidad* 5 (24) (May–June): 10–13.

Brockett, Charles D. 1991. "The Structure of Political Opportunities and Peasant Mobilization in Central America." *Comparative Politics* 23 (April): 253–74.

Burdick, John, Philip Oxhorn, and Kenneth M. Roberts, eds. 2009. *Beyond Neoliberalism in Latin America? Societies and Politics at the Crossroads.* New York: Palgrave Macmillan.

Caballero Martin, Víctor, and Teresa Cabrera Espinoza. 2008. "Conflictos sociales en el Perú, 2006–2008." In Toche Medrano 2008, 99–130.

Cameron, Maxwell A. 1994. *Democracy and Authoritarianism in Peru: Political Coalitions and Social Change.* New York: St. Martin's Press.

Cameron, Maxwell A. 2011a. "Peru: The Left Turn That Wasn't." In Steven Levitsky and Kenneth M. Roberts, eds., *The Resurgence of the Latin American Left.* Baltimore: John Hopkins University Press. 375–98.

Cameron, Maxwell A. 2011b. "Text, Power and Social Exclusion: From Colonialism to the Crisis of the Criollo Republicanism." In Crabtree 2011, 23–51.

Cameron, Maxwell A., and Philip Mauceri, eds. 1997. *The Peruvian Labyrinth: Polity, Society, Economy.* University Park: Pennsylvania State University Press.

Canessa Montejo, Miguel F. 2011. "La violencia política en el mundo laboral peruano." *Debates en Sociología* 36: 85–106.

Carrión, Julio F., ed. 2006. *The Fujimori Legacy: The Rise of Electoral Authoritarianism in Peru.* University Park: Pennsylvania State University Press.

Cheibub, José Antonio, Jennifer Gandhi, and James Raymond Vreeland. 2010. "Democracy and Dictatorship Revisited." *Public Choice* 143: 67–101.

Chhibber, Pradeep, and Irfan Nooruddin. 2004. "Do Party Systems Count? The Number of Parties and Government Performance in the Indian States." *Comparative Political Studies* 37 (2): 152–87.

Cingranelli, David L., and David L. Richards. 2010. "The Cingranelli and Richards (CIRI) Human Rights Data Project." *Human Rights Quarterly* 32 (2): 401–24.

Cleary, Matthew R. 2006. "Explaining the Left's Resurgence." *Journal of Democracy* 17 (4): 35–49.

Cleary, Matthew R. 2010. *The Sources of Democratic Responsiveness in Mexico.* South Bend, IN: University of Notre Dame Press.

Colburn, Forrest D. 2002. *Latin America at the End of Politics.* Princeton, NJ: Princeton University Press.

Collier, David, ed. 1979. *The New Authoritarianism in Latin America.* Princeton, NJ: Princeton University Press.

Collier, Paul, and Anke Hoeffler. 2002. "On the Incidence of Civil War in Africa." *Journal of Conflict Resolution* 46 (1): 13–28.

Collier, Paul, and Anke Hoeffler. 2005. "Resource Rents, Governance and Conflict." *Journal of Conflict Resolution* 49 (4): 625–33.

Collier, Ruth Berins, and David Collier. 1991. *Shaping the Political Arena: Critical Junctures, the Labor Movement, and Regime Dynamics in Latin America.* Princeton, NJ: Princeton University Press.

Comisión de la Verdad y Reconciliación. 2003. *Informe final.* Lima: Comisión de la Verdad y Reconciliación.

Conaghan, Catherine M. 2002. "Cashing In on Authoritarianism: Media Collusion in Fujimori's Peru." *Harvard International Journal of Press/Politics* 7 (1): 115–25.

Conaghan, Catherine M. 2005. *Fujimori's Peru: Deception in the Public Sphere.* Pittsburgh: University of Pittsburgh Press.

Cook, Maria Lorena. 1996. *Organizing Dissent: Unions, the State, and the Democratic Teachers' Movement in Mexico.* University Park: Pennsylvania State University Press.

CooperAcción. 2005. "Mapa nacional de concesiones mineras del Perú." Lima: CooperAcción. February.

CooperAcción. 2011. "Mapa de concesiones mineras del Perú." Lima: CooperAcción. November.

CooperAcción. 2013. "Mapa de concesiones mineras del Perú." Lima: CooperAcción. June.

Cotler, Julio. 2011. "Capitalismo y democracia en el Perú: La tentación autoritaria." In Luis Pásara, ed., *Perú: Ante los desafíos del siglo XXI.* Lima: Fondo Editorial de la Pontifica Universidad Católica del Perú. 519–55.

Crabtree, John, ed. 2011. *Fractured Politics: Peruvian Democracy Past and Present.* London: University of London, Institute for the Study of the Americas.

Cress, Daniel M., and David A. Snow. 2000. "The Outcomes of Homeless Mobilization: The Influence of Organization, Disruption, Political Mediation, and Framing." *American Journal of Sociology* 105 (January): 1063–104.

Crozier, Michel J., Samuel P. Huntington, and Joji Watanuki. 1975. *The Crisis of Democracy: Report on the Governability to the Trilateral Commission.* New York: New York University Press.

Davies, James C. 1962. "Toward a Theory of Revolution." *American Sociological Review* 27 (1): 5–19.

Davies, James C. 1969. "The J-Curve of Rising and Declining Satisfactions as a Cause of Some Great Revolutions and a Contained Rebellion." In T. R. Gurr and H. D. Graham, eds., *Violence in America*. New York: Praeger. 690–730.

De Echave, José, Alejandro Diez, Ludwig Huber, Bruno Revesz, Xavier Ricard Lanata, and Martín Tanaka. 2009. *Minería y conflicto social*. Lima: Instituto de Estudios Peruanos.

Defensoría del Pueblo. 2009. "Actuaciones humanitarias realizadas por la Defensoría del Pueblo con ocasión de los hechos ocurridos el 5 de junio del 2009, en las provincias de Utcubamba y Bagua, región Amazonas, en el contexto del paro amazónico." Informe de adjuntía Nro. 006. Lima: Defensoría del Pueblo.

Defensoría del Pueblo. 2012. "Reporte de conflictos sociales Nro. 100." Lima: Defensoría del Pueblo, Adjuntía para la Prevención de Conflictos Sociales y la Gobernabilidad.

Dietz, Henry A., and David J. Myers. 2007. "From Thaw to Deluge: Party System Collapse in Venezuela and Peru." *Latin American Politics and Society* 49 (2): 59–86.

Domínguez, Jorge I., and Michael Shifter, eds. 2013. *Constructing Democratic Governance in Latin America*. 4th ed. Baltimore: Johns Hopkins University Press.

Dreher, Axel, Noel Gaston, and Pim Martens. 2008. *Measuring Globalisation: Gauging Its Consequences*. New York: Springer.

Dunning, Thad. 2005. "Resource Dependence, Economic Performance, and Political Stability." *Journal of Conflict Resolution* 49 (4): 451–82.

Eisinger, Peter. 1973. "The Conditions of Protest Behavior in American Cities." *American Journal of Political Science* 67 (1): 11–28.

Falla Lamadrid, Luis Humberto, and Wilder Calderón Castro. 2010. *Informe en Minoría*. Lima: Congreso de la República, Comisión investigadora sobre los hechos acontecidos en la ciudad de Bagua, aledaños y otros, determinando responsabilidades a que haya lugar.

Fearon, James. 2005. "Primary Commodity Exports and Civil War." *Journal of Conflict Resolution* 49 (4): 483–507.

Fiorina, Morris P. 1981. *Retrospective Voting in American National Elections*. New Haven, CT: Yale University Press.

Francisco, Ronald A. 2009. *Dynamics of Conflict*. New York: Springer.

Gamson, William A., and David S. Meyer. 1996. "Framing Political Opportunity." In McAdam, McCarthy, and Zald 1996, 275–90.

García, María Elena. 2005. *Making Indigenous Citizens: Identity, Development, and Multicultural Activism in Peru*. Stanford, CA: Stanford University Press.

García, Mariel. 2010. "La democracia extractiva: Estado, corporaciones y comunidades en el caso Majaz." Lima: Informe final de beca CLACSO. Unpublished manuscript.

García, Mariel. 2011. "Gobernar al decretazo: Los peruanos del hortelano y los límites del modelo de Alan García." In Alfaro et al. 2011, 185–204.

Giugni, Marco, Douglas McAdam, and Charles Tilly, eds. 1998. *From Contention to Democracy*. Lanham, MD: Rowman and Littlefield.

Gonzales de Olarte, Efraín. 2000. *Neocentralismo y neoliberalismo en el Perú*. Lima: Instituto de Estudios Peruanos.

Goodwin, Jeff, and James M. Jasper, eds. 2003. *The Social Movements Reader: Cases and Concepts*. Oxford: Blackwell Publishers.

Goodwin, Jeff, and James M. Jasper, eds. 2004. *Rethinking Social Movements: Structure, Meaning, and Emotion*. Lanham, MD: Rowman and Littlefield.

Greene, Shane. 2006. "Getting over the Andes: The Geo-Eco-Politics of Indigenous Movements in Peru's Twenty-First Century Inca Empire." *Journal of Latin American Studies* 38 (2): 327–54.

Gurmendi, Alfredo C. 2008. "The Mineral Industry of Peru." In *U.S. Geological Survey Minerals Yearbook 2008*. US Department of the Interior: US Geological Survey, 16.1–16.13.

Haarstad, Håvard, and Arnt Fløysand. 2007. "Globalization and the Power of Rescaled Narratives: A Case of Opposition to Mining in Tambogrande, Peru." *Political Geography* 26 (3): 289–308.

Harvey, David. 2003. *The New Imperialism*. Oxford and New York: Oxford University Press.

Hecock, R. Douglas. 2006. "Electoral Competition, Globalization, and Subnational Education Spending in Mexico, 1999–2004." *American Journal of Political Science* 50 (4): 950–61.

Hochstetler, Kathryn. 2006. "Rethinking Presidentialism: Challenges and Presidential Falls in South America." *Comparative Politics* 38 (July): 401–18.

Holzner, Claudio A. 2007. "The Poverty of Democracy: Neoliberal Reforms and Political Participation of the Poor in Mexico." *Latin American Politics and Society* 49 (2): 87–122.

Humphreys, Macartan. 2005. "Natural Resources, Conflict, and Conflict Resolution: Uncovering the Mechanisms." *Journal of Conflict Resolution* 49 (4): 508–37.

Instituto Nacional de Estadística e Informática (INEI). 2011. *Peru: Compendio Estadístico 2011*. Lima: Instituto Nacional de Estadística e Informática.

Ipsos Apoyo. 2009. "Opinión Data: Resumen de Encuestas a la Opinión Pública." Lima: Ipsos Apoyo. June.

Isla Rojas, Víctor. 2010. *Informe en Minoría*. Lima: Congreso de la República, Comisión investigadora sobre los hechos acontecidos en la ciudad de Bagua, aledaños y otros, determinando responsabilidades a que haya lugar.

Jenkins, J. Craig, and Charles Perrow. 1977. "Insurgency of the Powerless: Farm Worker Movements (1946–1976)." *American Sociological Review* 42 (April): 249–68.

Karl, Terry Lynn. 1997. *The Paradox of Plenty: Oil Booms and Petro-States*. Berkeley: University of California Press.

Key, V. O., Jr. 1966. *The Responsible Electorate: Rationality in Presidential Voting, 1936–1960*. Cambridge, MA: Harvard University Press.

King, Gary, Michael Tomz, and Jason Wittenberg. 2000. "Making the Most of Statistical Analysis." *American Journal of Political Science* 44 (2): 347–61.

Kitschelt, Herbert P. 1986. "Political Opportunity Structures and Political Protest: Anti-Nuclear Movements in Four Democracies." *British Journal of Political Science* 16 (1): 57–85.

Kitschelt, Herbert, Kirk A. Hawkins, Juan Pablo Luna, Guillermo Rosas, and Elizabeth J. Zechmeister. 2010. *Latin American Party Systems*. New York: Cambridge University Press.

Koopmans, Ruud. 1995. "The Dynamics of Protest Waves." In Hanspeter Kriesi, Ruud Koopmans, Jan Willem Duyvendak, and Marco G. Giugni, eds., *New Social Movements in Western Europe: A Comparative Analysis*. Minneapolis: University of Minnesota Press. 111–42.

Kotschwar, Barbara, Theodore H. Moran, and Julia Muir. 2012. "Chinese Investment in Latin American Resources: The Good, the Bad, and the Ugly." Working paper, Peterson Institute for International Economics, Washington, DC.

Kruijt, Dirk, and Menno Vellinga. 1979. *Labor Relations and Multinational Corporations: The Cerro de Pasco Corporation in Peru (1902–1974)*. The Netherlands: Van Gorcum Press.

Kurtz, Marcus J. 2004. "The Dilemmas of Democracy in the Open Economy: Lessons from Latin America." *World Politics* 56 (2): 262–302.

Laakso, Markku, and Rein Taagepera. 1979. "Effective Number of Parties: A Measure with Application to Western Europe." *Comparative Political Studies* 12 (1): 3–27.

Latin American Public Opinion Projecty (LAPOP). 2008. *AmericasBarometer 2008*. Nashville: Vanderbilt University.

Latinobarómetro. 2009. *Latinobarómetro 2009*. Chile: Santiago de Chile.

Levitsky, Steven. 1999. "Fujimori and Post-Party Politics in Peru." *Journal of Democracy* 10 (3): 78–92.

Levitsky, Steven. 2013. "Peru: The Challenges of a Democracy without Parties." In Domínguez and Shifter 2013, 282–315.

Levitsky, Steven, and Maxwell A. Cameron. 2003. "Democracy without Parties? Political Parties and Regime Change in Fujimori's Peru." *Latin American Politics and Society* 45 (3): 1–34.

Lingán, Jeannet. 2008. "El caso de Cajamarca." In Scurrah 2008, 31–68.

Llona, Mariana. 2008. "El gobierno aprista y las ONG: Un nuevo ciclo de disputa por los derechos." In Toche Medrano 2008, 131–58.

Lombardi Elías, Guido. 2010. *Informe en Minoría*. Lima: Congreso de la República, Comisión investigadora sobre los hechos acontecidos en la ciudad de Bagua, aledaños y otros, determinando responsabilidades a que haya lugar.

Long, J. Scott. 1997. *Regression Models for Categorical and Limited Dependent Variables*. Thousand Oaks, CA: Sage Publications.

Lowrie, Nola D. 2002. "Tambogrande: A Case Study of Conflict over the Use of Natural Resources and the Allocation of Risk." Research Paper for the Degree of Master of Regional Planning, Cornell University.

Machado, Fabiana, Carlos Scartascini, and Mariano Tommasi. 2009. *Political Institutions and Street Protests in Latin America*. Working paper 110, Inter-American Development Bank, Washington, DC.

Mainwaring, Scott, Daniel Brinks, and Aníbal Pérez-Liñán. 2001. "Classifying Political Regimes in Latin America." *Studies in Comparative International Development* 36 (1): 37–65.

Marshall, Monty G., and K. Jaggers. 2009. *Polity IV Project: Dataset Users' Manual*. Severn, MD: Center for Systematic Peace.

Mauceri, Philip. 1995. "State Reform, Coalitions, and the Neoliberal Autogolpe in Peru." *Latin American Research Review* 30 (1): 7–37.

Mazzuca, Sebastián. 2013. "Natural Resources Boom and Institutional Curses in the New Political Economy in South America." In Domínguez and Shifter 2013, 102–26.

McAdam, Doug. 1982. *Political Process and the Development of Black Insurgency, 1930–1970*. Chicago: University of Chicago Press.

McAdam, Doug. 1996. "Conceptual Origins, Current Problems and Future Directions." In McAdam, McCarthy, and Zald 1996, 23–40.

McAdam, Doug, John D. McCarthy, and Mayer N. Zald, eds. 1996. *Comparative Perspectives on Social Movements: Political Opportunities, Mobilizing Structures, and Cultural Framings*. Cambridge: Cambridge University Press.

McAdam, Doug, Sidney Tarrow, and Charles Tilly. 2001. *Dynamics of Contention*. Cambridge: Cambridge University Press.

McCarthy, John D., and Mayer N. Zald. 1997. "Resource Mobilization and Social Movements: A Partial Theory." *American Journal of Sociology* 82 (6): 1212–41.

McClintock, Cynthia. 1998. *Revolutionary Movements in Latin America: El Salvador's FMLN and Peru's Shining Path*. Washington, DC: United States Institute of Peace Press.

McMillan, John, and Pablo Zoido. 2004. "How to Subvert Democracy: Montesinos in Peru." *Journal of Economic Perspectives* 18 (4): 69–92.

McNulty, Stephanie L. 2011. *Voice and Vote: Decentralization and Participation in Post-Fujimori Peru*. Stanford, CA: Stanford University Press.

Meléndez, Carlos. 2005. "Mediaciones y conflictos: Las transformaciones de la intermediación política y los estallidos de violencia en el Perú actual." In Víctor Vich, ed., *El Estado está de vuelta: Desigualdad, diversidad, y democracia*. Lima, Peru: Instituto de Estudios Peruanos. 159–83.

Meléndez, Carlos. 2009. "Movilización sin movimientos. El caso de los conflictos entre comunidades y la empresa minera Yanacocha en Cajamarca." In Romeo Grompone and Martín Tanaka, eds., *Entre el crecimiento económico y la insatisfacción social: Las protestas sociales en el Perú actual*. Peru: Instituto de Estudios Peruanos. 321–80.

Meléndez, Carlos, and Carlos León. 2009. "Perú 2008: El juego de ajedrez de la gobernabilidad en partidas simultáneas." *Revista de ciencia politica* 29 (2): 591–609.

Meléndez, Carlos, and Carlos León. 2010. "Perú 2009: Los legados del autoritarismo." *Revista de ciencia política* 30 (2): 451–77.

Meyer, David. 2004. "Protest and Political Opportunities." *Annual Review of Sociology* 30 (21): 125–45.

Ministerio de Energía y Minas (MEM). 2004. *Anuario Minero 2004*. Lima: Ministerio de Energía y Minas.

Ministerio de Energía y Minas (MEM). 2010. *Anuario Minero 2010*. Lima: Ministerio de Energía y Minas.

Monge, Carlos, Claudia Viale, and Felipe Bedoya. 2011. "Las industrias extractivas con Alan García y los retos de Ollanta Humala." In Alfaro et al. 2011, 305–31.

Monning, William W. 2005. "The Treasure of Cajamarca—and Other Peruvian Curses." *NACLA Report on the Americas* (March–April).

Morley, Samuel, Roberto Machado, and Stefano Pettinato. 1999. *Indexes of Structural Reform in Latin America*. Santiago, Chile: Economic Commission for Latin America and the Caribbean.

Moyano Delgado, Martha, Eduardo Espinoza Ramos, and Juan Perry Cruz. 2010. *Informe en Mayoría*. Lima: Congreso de la República, Comisión investigadora sobre los hechos acontecidos en la ciudad de Bagua, aledaños y otros, determinando responsabilidades a que haya lugar.

Muñoz Portugal, Ismael. 2009. "Acción colectiva, desigualdad y conflicto en la sociedad peruana: Una aproximación." Unpublished manuscript, Escuela de Gobierno y Políticas Públicas, Pontificia Universidad Católica del Perú, Lima.

Muradian, Roldan, Joan Martinez-Alier, and Humberto Correa. 2003. "International Capital versus Local Population: The Environmental Conflict of the Tambogrande Mining Project, Peru." *Society and Natural Resources* 1 (6): 775–92.

Murillo, Maria Victoria, and Lucas Ronconi. 2004. "Teacher's Strikes in Argentina: Partisan Alignments and Public-Sector Labor Relations." *Studies in Comparative International Development* 39 (1): 77–98.

Norris, Pippa, Stefaan Walgrave, and Peter Van Aelst. 2005. "Who Demonstrates? Antistate Rebels, Conventional Participants, or Everyone?" *Comparative Politics* 37 (2): 189–205.

Obando, Enrique. 1998. "Civil-Military Relations in Peru, 1980–1996: How to Control and Coopt the Military (and the Consequences of Doing So)." In Steve Stern, ed., *Shining and Other Paths: War and Society in Peru, 1980–1995*. Durham, NC: Duke University Press. 384–410.

O'Donnell, Guillermo A. 1973. *Modernization and Bureaucratic-Authoritarianism: Studies in South American Politics*. Berkeley, CA: Institute of International Studies.

Oficina Nacional de Procesos Electorales (ONPE). 2012. "Información Electoral." Lima: Oficina Nacional de Procesos Electorales. http://www.web.onpe.gob.pe/.

References　　　155

Ohmae, Kenichi. 1995. *The End of the Nation State: The Rise of Regional Economics.* London: Harper Collins.

Oxfam America. 2001. *An Alternative Look at a Proposed Mine in Tambogrande, Peru.* Washington DC: Oxfam America, Mineral Policy Center, and Vancouver, Canada: Environmental Mining Council of British Columbia.

Oxfam America. 2009. *Conflictos mineros en el Perú: Condición crítica.* United Kingdom: Oxfam International.

Oxhorn, Phillip. 2006. "Neopluralism and the Challenges for Citizenship in Latin America." In Joseph S. Tulchin and Margaret Ruthenberg, eds., *Citizenship in Latin America.* Boulder, CO: Lynne Rienner Publishers. 123–47.

Oxhorn, Phillip. 2009. "Beyond Neoliberalism? Latin America's New Crossroads." In Burdick, Oxhorn, and Roberts 2009, 217–34.

Oxhorn, Philip D., and Graciela Ducantenzeiler, eds. 1998. *What Kind of Democracy? What Kind of Market? Latin America in the Age of Neoliberalism.* University Park: Pennsylvania State University Press.

Pajuelo, Ramón. 2010. "Los mineros de la Sierra Central y la masacre de Malpaso: Apuntes para una lectura retrospectiva." In Alberto Flores Galindo et al., eds., *Jorge del Prado y los mineros de la Sierra Central: Testimonio sobre la masacre de Malpaso.* Lima: Fondo Editorial del Congreso del Perú. 213–32.

Palmer, David Scott, ed. 1992. *Shining Path of Peru.* New York: St. Martin's Press.

Paredes, Martiza. 2008. "El caso de Tambogrande." In Scurrah 2008, 268–300.

Paredes, Martiza. 2011. "Indigenous Politics and the Legacy of the Left." In Crabtree 2011, 129–57.

Perreault, Thomas. 2006. "From the Guerra Del Agua to the Guerra Del Gas: Resource Governance, Neoliberalism and Popular Protest in Bolivia." *Antipode* 38: 150–72.

Piven, Frances F., and Richard A. Cloward. 1979. *Poor People's Movements.* New York: Vintage.

Pizarro, Rosa, Laura Trelles, and Eduardo Toche. 2004. "La protesta social durante el Toledismo." In Azpur et. al. 2004, 27–100.

Przeworski, Adam, and Fernando Limongi. 1993. "Political Regimes and Economic Growth." *Journal of Economic Perspectives* 7 (Summer): 51–69.

Raymond, Christopher, and Moisés Arce. 2013. "The Politicization of Indigenous Identities in Peru." *Party Politics* 19 (4): 555–76.

Remy, María Isabel S. 2010. "El asedio desde los márgenes: Entre la multiplicidad de conflictos locales y la lenta formación de nuevos movimientos sociales en Perú." In Martín Tanaka and Francine Jácome, eds., *Desafíos de la gobernabilidad democrática: Reformas político-institucionales y movimientos sociales en la región andina.* Lima: Instituto de Estudios Peruanos. 277–312.

Rénique, Gerardo. 2009. "Against the Law of the Jungle: Peru's Amazonian Uprising." *NACLA Report on the Americas* (January–February).

Reymundo Mercado, Edgard, and Róger Nájar Kokally. 2011. *Más allá de la*

Curva del Diablo: Lecciones de Bagua. Lima: Fondo Editorial del Congreso del Perú.

Rice, Roberta. 2012. *The New Politics of Protest: Indigenous Mobilization in Latin America's Neoliberal Era.* Tucson: University of Arizona Press.

Roberts, Bryan R., and Alejandro Portes. 2006. "Coping with the Free Market City: Collective Action in Six Latin American Cities at the End of the Twentieth Century." *Latin American Research Review* 41 (2): 57–83.

Roberts, Kenneth M. 2002. "Social Inequalities without Class Cleavages in Latin America's Neoliberal Era." *Studies in Comparative International Development* 36 (4): 3–33.

Roberts, Kenneth M. 2008. "The Mobilization of Opposition to Economic Liberalization." *Annual Review of Political Science* 11 (1): 327–49.

Robertson, Graeme B., and Emmanuel Teitelbaum. 2011. "Foreign Direct Investment, Regime Type, and Labor Protest in Developing Countries." *American Journal of Political Science* 55 (3): 665–77.

Rokkan, Stein. 1970. *Citizens, Elections, Parties: Approaches to the Comparative Study of the Processes of Development.* New York: David McKay Company.

Ross, Michael. 1999. "The Political Economy of the Resource Curse." *World Politics* 51 (2): 297–322.

Salas Rodríguez, Iván. 2006. *Quilish Hora Cero: Cajamarca, la lucha de un pueblo que defiende su vida y dignidad.* Cajamarca, Peru.

Scott, James C. 1986. *Weapons of the Weak: Everyday Forms of Peasant Resistance.* New Haven, CT: Yale University Press.

Scurrah, Martín, ed. 2008. *Defendiendo derechos y promoviendo cambios. El estado, las empresas extractivas y las comunidades locales en el Perú.* Lima: Instituto de Estudios Peruanos.

Seifert, Manuel. 2011. "Colapso de los partidos nacionales y auge de los partidos regionales: Las elecciones regionales 2002–2010." MA thesis, Pontificia Universidad Católica del Perú, Lima.

Selby, Jan. 2005. "Oil and Water: The Contrasting Anatomies of Resource Conflicts." *Government and Opposition* 40: 200–224.

Silva, Eduardo. 2009. *Challenging Neoliberalism in Latin America.* New York: Cambridge University Press.

Silver, Beverley. 2003. *Forces of Labor: Worker's Movements and Globalization since 1870.* Cambridge: Cambridge University Press.

Slack, Keith. 2009. "Digging Out from Neoliberalism: Responses to Environmental (Mis)governance of the Mining Sector in Latin America." In Burdick, Oxhorn, and Roberts 2009, 117–34.

Snow, David, and Robert Benford. 1988. "Ideology, Frame Resonance, and Participant Mobilization." *International Social Movement Research* 26 (1): 197–217.

Snyder, Richard. 2001. "Scaling Down: The Subnational Comparative Method." *Studies in Comparative International Development* 36 (Spring): 93–110.

Stetson, George. 2010. "Hydrocarbon Conflict in the Peruvian Amazon: Indigenous Peoples' Decolonization of Development and Sustainability." PhD dissertation, Colorado State University.

Strange, Susan. 1996. *The Retreat of the State: The Diffusion of Power in the World Economy.* Cambridge: Cambridge University Press.

Tanaka, Martín, and Sofía Vera. 2008. "El 'neodualismo' de la política peruana." *Revista de ciencia política* 28 (1): 347–65.

Tarrow, Sidney. 1998. *Power in Movement: Social Movements and Contentious Politics.* Cambridge: Cambridge University Press.

Thorp, Rosemary. 2012. "The Challenges of Mining-Based Development in Peru." In Rosemary Thorp, Stefania Battistelli, Yvan Guichaoua, José Carlos Orihuela, and Maritza Paredes, eds., *The Developmental Challenges of Mining and Oil: Lessons from Africa and Latin America.* New York: Palgrave MacMillan. 110–30.

Thorp, Rosemary, and Geoffrey Bertram. 1978. *Peru, 1890–1977: Growth and Policy in an Open Economy.* London: Palgrave Macmillan.

Tilly, Charles. 1978. *From Mobilization to Revolution.* New York: Random House.

Tilly, Charles, and Sidney Tarrow. 2006. *Contentious Politics.* Boulder, CO: Paradigm Publishers.

Toche Medrano, Eduardo, ed. 2008. *Perú hoy: Por aquí compañeros, Aprismo y neoliberalismo.* Lima: DESCO.

Vergara, Alberto. 2011. "United by Discord, Divided by Consensus: National and Sub-National Articulation in Bolivia and Peru, 2000–2010." *Journal of Latin American Politics* 3: 65–93.

Walton, John, and David Seddon. 1994. *Free Markets and Food Riots: The Politics of Global Adjustment.* Oxford, UK: Blackwell.

Weyland, Kurt. 2002. *The Politics of Market Reform in Fragile Democracies: Argentina, Brazil, Peru, and Venezuela.* Princeton, NJ: Princeton University Press.

Weyland, Kurt. 2009. "The Rise of Latin America's Two Lefts: Insights from Rentier State Theory." *Comparative Politics* 4 (2): 145–64.

Wibbels, Erik. 2004. "Decentralization, Democracy, and Market Reform: On the Difficulties of Killing Two Birds with One Stone." In Alfred P. Montero and David J. Samuels, eds., *Decentralization and Democracy in Latin America.* Notre Dame, IN: University of Notre Dame Press. 203–34.

Wilkinson, Steven. 2004. *Votes and Violence: Electoral Competition and Ethnic Riots in India.* Cambridge: Cambridge University Press.

Yashar, Deborah J. 1998. "Contesting Citizenship: Indigenous Movements and Democracy in Latin America." *Comparative Politics* 31 (October): 23–42.

Zald, Mayer N. 1996. "Culture, Ideology, and Strategic Framing." In McAdam, McCarthy, and Zald 1996, 261–74.

Zavalla, Cynthia. 2004. "Canon minero y distribución de ingresos en el Perú." In Azpur et. al. 2004, 149–92.

Zermeño, Sergio. 1990. "Crisis, Neoliberalism, and Disorder." In Joe Foreweraker and Ann L. Craig, eds., *Popular Movements and Political Change in Mexico.* Boulder, CO: Lynne Rienner. 160–82.

INDEX

Note: Page numbers in *italic* refer to figures and tables.

COICA. *See* Coordinator of Indigenous Organizations of the Amazon Basin

Colburn, Forrest, end of politics and, 40

collective action, xvi–xvii, xix, 9, 10, 14, 119; decline in, 6; economic liberalization and, 7; resource mobilization and, 23; successful, 8

collective power, 14, 71–72, 75–78, 91, 98–102, 118; building, xix, 38; weak, 23

Colom, Alvaro, 125

Comando Rodrigo Franco (CRF), 128

Comisión Episcopal de Acción Social, 142n8

Committee on Energy and Mines (Comisión de Energía y Minas), 96

Common Good Institute (Instituto del Bien Común [IBC]), alternative report and, 116

Compañía de Minas Buenaventura, 87, 97–98

Compañía Minera Antamina, 145n9

competition, 20, 21; democracy and, 25; responsiveness and, xviii; subnational, 32. *See also* political competition

Compliance Advisor Ombudsman (CAO), 99, 100, 143n10

CONACAMI. *See* National Confederation of Peruvian Communities Affected by Mining

CONAP. *See* Confederation of Amazonian Nationalities of Peru

concessions, 71, 95, 125; private companies and, *47*

Condor Mountain Range National Park, 108

Confederation of Amazonian Nationalities of Peru (Confederación de Nacionalidades Amazónicas del Perú [CONAP]), 116; AIDESEP and, 109; roundtable and, 109

CONFIEP. *See* National Confederation of Private Business Institutions

consultation mechanism, 50, 71, 73, 79, 117

contention, *41*, 45, 49, 57; antimarket, xiii–

xiv, xviii, 40, 64, 106; anti-neoliberal, 14; cycle of, xxii; democratizing consequences of, xxiv; political consequences of, xv; subnational, xiii, xxiv; waves/modes of, xxii, 40

Convention 169 (C169) (ILO), xxiii, 108, 116–18, 125; implementation of, 115, 118

CooperAcción, 104, 142n8

Coordinadora Nacional de Derechos Humanos, 142n8

Coordinator of Indigenous Organizations of the Amazon Basin (Coordinadora de las Organizaciones Indígenas de la Cuenca Amazónica [COICA]), 118; AIDESEP and, 107

copper, 48, 49, 69

Corral Quemado, blocking, 108

Cotler, Julio, 131

Council on Hemispheric Affairs, 114

CPC. *See* Cerro de Pasco Corporation

Crabtree, John, 105

cross-national studies, 13, 14

Cross-National Time Series (CNTS), 13, 139n8

CTAR. *See* Transitional Regional Board

Cuajone mine, 105

cultural identity, 70, 74, 76, 103, 125, 144n9

cyanide, 77, 88

DAR. *See* Law, Environment, and Natural Resources

Davies, James, theory of, 9

decentralization, 60, 64; consequence of, 55; mineral rents and, *60*; political representation and, 54; politics of, 53; process, xv, 31–32, 49, 54, 59, 61, 146n13

Declaration of Machu Picchu, 140n8

Deep Peru (Perú profundo), 31

defense fronts (frentes de defensa), 42

Del Castillo, Jorge, 113

demands, types of, 133, 135–36

demands for rights, 24, 50–51, 53, 54, 106–8, 141n3

demands for services, 24, 50, 51–54, 141n3
demobilization, xiv, xxii, 28, 37, 57; democracy and, 27; mobilization and, 43
democracy: autocracy and, xvii; competition and, 25; conceptualization of, xvii, 11–12, 14–15, 25, 44; demobilization and, 27; economic liberalization and, 119; electoral theories of, xvii, 19; free markets and, 25; global struggles for, 77; government responsiveness and, xviii; grassroots, 23, 82; market-era, 4–5; mobilization and, xvii, 19, 21, 27, 121; Peru and, 28–30; political opportunities and, 46; protests and, xvii, 5, 9; repoliticization and, 39–44; transition to, xxii, 15, 24–25, 27; weak institutions and, xvi–xvii. *See also* political democracy
democratization, xvii, 18; macro political opportunities and, 11
depoliticization perspective, 4, 138n3; economic liberalization and, 5–7; free markets/democracy and, 25
Devéscovi Dzierzón, Jose Luis, 96
Devil's Curve, 112, 113
Diaconía para la Justicia y la Paz de Piura, 142n8
disappearances, 39
disruptive strategies, 19, 74, 122
distributive justice, 53, 54, 58, 63
DL. *See* legislative decrees
Doe Run, Centromín Peru and, 145n8
dog in the manger syndrome, 104–6

ECO, 142n8
economic conditions, 5, 6, 12, 17, 38, 43, 54, 140n12
economic crisis, 4, 46, 106, 138n6
economic decline, 28, 33, 37
economic growth, xv, 27, 31, 33, 35, 45, 70, 106, 129; mining and, 48; sustaining, 64
economic liberalization, xii, xiv, 9, 10, 17, 21, 32, 47, 104, 125–26; challenging, 3, 5, 13, 138n3; consequences of, xviii, xx, xxi, 3, 5, 6, 13, 14, 15, 40; contentious

politics and, 13; demobilizing effects of, 43; democracy and, 119; depoliticization and, 5–7; described, xi; development of, xxii, 106; disorganizing effects of, 5; end of politics and, 25; general response to, 14; grievances/threats from, xiii; impersonal forces of, 4; as master frame, 12; mining companies and, 59; national outcomes and, 42; policies, xii, xiv, 3, 38, 45, 128; political democracy and, 11, 13, 14; repoliticization and, 13, 16, 43; strategic framing and, 12; sustainability of, xxiii; transition toward, 24–25; uneven benefits of, 129
economic performance, 19, 38
economic policies, xi, 4, 14, 29
economic reform, xviii, 4, 14, 25, 138n3
economic threats, xxi, 3, 14, 119
Economist, 37
Ecovida, 89, 99
Ecumenical Foundation for Development and Peace (Federación Ecuménica para el Desarrollo y la Paz [FEDEPAZ]), 86, 142n8
effective number of parties (ENP), 55, 102, 141n10
EIA. *See* environmental impact report
El Comercio, 105, 133, 134, 138n10; editorials in, 129
El Correo, 81
El Expreso, 133, 134
El Milagro, 95
El Niño, 142n1, 143n10
El Tiempo, 81
EMSE, Osisko and, 124
ENP. *See* effective number of parties
environmental assessments, 51, 100
environmental concerns, 23, 24, 50, 76, 77, 79, 106, 125, 127, 136
environmental impact report (*estudio de impacto ambiental* [EIA]), 73, 93, 101, 123, 142n6
Environmental Mining Council of British Columbia, 143n9
Espinoza, Eduardo, 115

European Union, 32
exports, 49, 99, *99*, 130
extractive economy, 101; bad news/good news of, 54; environmental oversight of, 50; expansion of, xii, 16–17, 104; protesting, 44, 49, 91, 117. *See also* mining; new mining; resource extraction

Falla, Luis, 115
FDVST. *See* San Lorenzo Valley and Tambogrande Defense Front
FEDEPAZ. *See* Ecumenical Foundation for Development and Peace
Fernández, Rosario, on Pizango, 112
Fleury, Hans, 74
FNTMMSP. *See* National Federation of Miners, Metal and Steel Workers of Peru
Forest and Wildlife Law (DL 1090), 110, 111, 112, 114
fragmentation, 18, 23–24, 36, 120; social, 131. *See also* political fragmentation
framing processes, 7, 9, 10, 12, 26, 65, 70
Freedom House, 40, 41, 140n13
free trade agreements (FTAs), 32, 34, 106, 115, 126, 129; economic liberalization and, 103
Frente Para la Victoria (FPV), 145n1
Friends of the Earth, 143n9
fronts, described, 135
FTAs. *See* free trade agreements
Fujimori, Alberto, xiv, xvii, 20, 34, 37, 39, 40, 49, 104, 106, 129; AF and, 103, 110; centralization and, 31; Centromín Perú and, 46; corruption of, 30, 133–34; downfall of, 30, 87, 91; economic liberalization and, 6, 32, 47, 59, 125–26; election of, 28–29, 30; FNTMMSP and, 46–47; foreign investment and, 47, 126; free press and, 134; mercury spill and, 89; mining and, 70; mobilization and, 30, 71; neoliberal reforms and, 139n2; Newmont and, 143n3; opposition to, 140n7; political violence and, 29–30; rise of, 44

Fujimori, Keiko, 33–34

Gana Perú (Peru Wins), 34
García, Alan, 115, 122, 133; AF and, 103; AIDESEP and, 107, 144n1; APRA and, 55, 110; bargaining roundtables and, 35; Convention 169 and, 116–17; decentralization process and, 146n13; decrees by, 118; development and, 105, 107–8; doctrinal maturity and, 105; economic collapse and, 33; economic growth and, 35; economic liberalization and, 32, 106; fiscal benefits and, 130; foreign investment policies and, 126; FTA and, 129; geological endowments and, 105; government of, 30, 64; Humala and, 34; Law of Prior Consultation and, 117; mobilization against, 37, 108–14; peace/reconciliation and, 114; personal redemption for, 130; Peruvian Left and, 128–29; policy initiatives of, 104; political strategy of, 34; protestors and, 113; subnational governments and, 31; Toledo and, 36; vision of, 132
García Baca, Godofredo, 73; death of, 74, 78–79
GDP, 29, 37, 58, 61, 140n12; drop in, 28; growth of, 32, 33, 64
General Confederation of Peruvian Workers (Confederación General de Trabajadores del Perú [GCTP]), 41–42
general public, described, 135
globalization, 14, 138n1, 138n7; backlash against, 3; end of politics and, 25
gold, 69, 71, 92; cyanide and, 88; export of, 99, *99*; mining, 84, 99; price of, 48, *92*
Goldcorp, 125
government responsiveness, xvii, xxi, 137n5; political competition and, ix, xviii, 120; source of, 19
Gran Minería, 126
grassroots organizations, xxiv, 75
grievances, xiii, xxi, 54, 119; political, 12; resource-based, xxiii, 61; resource extraction, 10

ness Institutions (Confederación Nacional de Instituciones Empresariales Privada [CONFIEP]), 104

National Coordinator for Human Rights in Peru (Coordinadora Nacional de Derechos Humanos [CNDDHH]), 114; alternative report and, 116

National Federation of Miners, Metal and Steel Workers of Peru (Federación Nacional de Trabajadores Mineros, Metalúrgicos y Siderúrgicos del Perú [FNTMMSP]), 42, 128; Fujimori and, 46–47

National Jury of Elections (JNE), 136

National Office of Electoral Processes (ONPE), 135, 136

National Society of Mining, Petroleum, and Energy (Sociedad Nacional de Minería, Petróleo y Energía [SNMPE]), 74, 79; new mining and, 78

National Truth Commission (National Truth and Reconciliation Commission), 30, 39, 128

Nationalist Party of Peru (PNP), 33, 113

natural resources, 65; abundance of, xiv, 45; efficient use of, 105; exploitation of, 50, 130; expropriation of, xvi; investment in, xii; protests over, 54

neoliberalism, 9, 104, 129, 138n6, 139n2; alternative to, 43; described, xi; governing practices of, 106; reforming, xii, xiv; resource extraction and, xiii; supporting, xxi

new mining, 16, 17, 82, 126, 128; response of, 78–79. *See also* extractive economy; mining; resource extraction

New York Times, 84

Newmont Mining Corporation, 87, 98, 143n3; complaints with, 86; Yanacocha and, 84

nongovernmental organizations (NGOs), xix, xxiv, 65, 82, 86, 90, 93, 99, 104; antimining, 22, 78; environmental, 16, 50; international, 76, 77; mining interests and, 79, 80; network of, 76; participa-

tion of, 22, 23; reports by, 76–77; resources from, 76

Normandy Poseidon, 87

Norwegian Agency for Development (NORAD), 144n9

Nouvelle Planette, 144n9

O'Donnell, Guillermo, economic crises and, 4

Office of the Ombudsman (Defensoría del Pueblo), 27, 35, 109, 115, 116, 141n2; June 5 mobilization and, 113

Official Peru (Perú oficial), 31

oil rents (*canon petrolero*), establishment of, 53

Ojeda Riofrío, Francisco ("Pancho"), 72, 75, 80; battle for Tambogrande and, 81; election of, 82–83

ONPE. *See* National Office of Electoral Processes

Ordinance 012, 93

Organization of American States (OAS), AIDESEP and, 144n9

organizational capacity, xix, 65, 75, 137n2

Osisko Mining Corporation, EMSE and, 124

outcomes, 39, 42; social, 19; typology of, *22*; understanding, 21

output, public preferences and, xviii, 20, 57

Oxfam, 22, 114, 144n9

Oxfam America, 76, 77, 116

Oxfam UK, 76, 77, 79, 90

País Posible, 140n4

Palacios, Mario, 107

Paniagua, Valentín, 30, 132, 142n5

Paro Amazónico, 110, 118

participation, xiv, 22, 23, 74–75, 90; political, 30–31, 138n2; popular, 11; rights, 50

Partido Justicialista (PJ), 145n1

Partido Nacionalista, 115

Peasant Confederation of Peru (Confederación Campesina del Perú [CCP]), alternative report and, 116

pension systems, privatization of, xi

demands of, 18; strategies for, 25–26; variation of, 10, 18, 39, 119

protests, xxii, *42*, 44, 60, 62, 102; antigovernment, 12, *12*; antimarket, xiii, xxi, 14; antimining, 75, 76, 81–82; contentious episodes and, 57; cyclical patterns of, 58; definition of, 137n1; democracy and, xvii, 5, 9; factors of, 17; geographic dispersion of, 36; in Latin America, *12*; levels of, 39; localized, 118; market-era, 4–5; mining and, 21, 49–54, 57, 63; as mobilization, 38; political, xi, xxiii, 64, 120, 137n1; political fragmentation/mineral rent and, *62*, *63*; referendum and, 71–73; segmentation of, 16; social, xiv, 27, 137n1; subnational variation of, 15, 17–21; targets of, 133, 136; trends in/explaining, 37–39; types of, 45–46, 133, 134–35

public preferences, government output and, xviii, 20, 57

public sector, described, 135

Quea, Felipe, 93, 95, 96

Quijandría, Jaime, 98, 101

Quilish, 96, 101, 110, 143n6; mobilization in, 91, 95, 98, 101; September outburst and, 91–93

Radio Programas del Perú (RPP), 113

Rain Forest Foundation, 144n9

Rainforest Alliance, 114

RANSA, 88, 89

referendum, 23; protests and, 71–73

regional elections, 49, 55, 57; multiparty environment of, 56; results for, *56*

regional fronts (*frentes regionales*), 42

regional government, 31, 32, 49; described, 136; introduction of, 60; mobilizations and, 35; parties representing, 55

regional movements (*movimientos regionales*), 32

regional politics, 54–57, 61; fragmented/fluid, 56, 64; protests and, 46, 64

Rengifo Navarrete, Alfredo, 73, 80

repoliticization perspective, 4, 5, 7–10, 11, 12, 13, 14, 25, 119; democracy and, 39–44; economic liberalization and, 16, 43; support of, 17

resource extraction, xvi, xix, xx, xxiii, 38, 53, 60, 120; economic importance of, 47; employment in, 78; expansion of, 45; impracticality of, 75; income from, 51; mobilizations over, xv, xx, xxiii, 22; national politics and, xxiv; neoliberalism and, xiii; protesting, 16, 21, 57, 63; revenues from, 52; stopping, 124–25. *See also* extractive economy; mining; new mining

resource governance, 55, 60, 64; improving, 54

resource mobilization, xvi, xix, xxii, xxiii, 7, 10, 26, 36, 65, 121; collective action and, 23

responsiveness, 20, 54, 57, 58; accountability and, 25, 61, 102. *See also* government responsiveness; policy responsiveness

Restauración Nacional-Alianza Nacional, 115

Río Grande, 91, 94, 96

Río Porcón, 86, 94, 96

riots, xiv; defining, 12; number of, *12*

roadblocks, 43, 90, 94, 95, 96–97; described, 134

Rodríguez, Orestes, 128

Rokkan, Stein, whole-nation bias and, xx

Roundtable for Poverty Reduction, 99

roundtables. *See* bargaining roundtables

rule of law, 19, 79

rural patrols (*rondas campesinas*), 93, 97

Saavedra, Lot, 89

San Lorenzo Valley and Tambogrande Defense Front (Frentes de Defensa del Valle de San Lorenzo y Tambogrande (FDVST), 70, 72, 73, 79; lime war and, 74

San Miguel Ixtahuacán, 125

Sánchez, Elena, 95

Sandoval, Saúl, assassination of, 128

scale-shift, xiv, 17, 24, 27, 98, 143n9

SCC. *See* Southern Copper Corporation

Scott, James C., xxi

self-determination, 77, 78, 79

September 2 conflict, 94–96

Shining Path (Sendero Luminoso), 28, 30, 38, 113, 128

Shougang Group, 126, 127, 145n10

Silva, Eduardo, xiv, xx, xxi, 138n6, 142n13; analysis by, 9, 14, 15, 34

Simon, Yehude, 114, 115

Sipacapa, 125

sit-ins, 43; described, 134

small farmers, described, 135

SNMPE. *See* National Society of Mining, Petroleum, and Energy

social construction, as framing processes, 8–9

social, described, 136

social forces, 4, 53

social inclusion, xxiv, 33, 34, 131–32

social movements, xvi, 7, 14, 18, 21, 138n5; development of, 8, 10; literature, 26, 36; protest movements and, 10

social problems, 35, 100

social responsibility, 100, 101; corporate, xxiv, 127

social services, xi, 9, 54, 127

societal organizations (*rondas campesinas*), 101

Sole Civic Committee for the Defense of Life and the Environment (Comité Cívico Unitario para la Defensa de la Vida y del Medio Ambiente), 97

Sole Union of Workers of Peruvian Education (Sindicato Único de Trabajadores de la Educación Peruana [SUTEP]), 42, 128

Southern Common Market (MERCOSUR), 32

Southern Copper Corporation (SCC), 82, 122–23, 145n6

Southern Peruvian Copper Corporation, 126, 145n6

Splett, David, 127

Stratus Consulting, 100

strikes, 72–73, 141n14; decline in, 128; described, 134; hunger, 134; in Latin America, *12*; level of, 41; in Peru, *42*; regional, 101

subnational comparative analysis, xix–xxiv, 57–59, 137n8; heterogeneity/complexity and, xx

subnational governments, 19, 31; public investment for, 49; representation/performance of, 102

subnational protests, xix, 15, 21, 59–60, 61; levels of, 26; national politics and, 11; regional politics and, 46

SUTEP. *See* Sole Union of Workers of Peruvian Education

takeover (*toma*), 43; described, 134

Tambo Valley Defense Front (Frente de Defensa del Valle del Tambo [FDVT]), 123

Tambogrande, 50, 73, 79, 85, 89, 91, 94; agriculture in, 22, 24, 78; associational power in, 71–72, 75–78; battle for, 70, 75, 81–82; collective power in, 71–72, 75–78; democracy and, 77; investments in, 69; mobilization in, xxiii, 69, 76, 80, 117; strike in, 72–73

TC. *See* Peruvian Constitutional Tribunal

Tecnificación de la Producción del Cuy como Alternativa Rentable, 143n11

Tía María, 82, 122, 123, 124

Toledo, Alejandro, 20, 34, 113, 133; bargaining roundtables and, 35; criticism of, 129; decentralization and, 31–32, 59, 60; economic growth and, 35, 64; economic liberalization and, 32; environmental issues and, 77; foreign investment policies and, 126; García and, 36; government of, 30; indigenous symbols of, 140n8; mining and, 70; National Truth and Reconciliation Commission and, 39; Perú Posible and, 55; reforms by, 31, 140n3

Torres Seoane, Javier, 141n3

townspeople, described, 135

Training and Intervention Group for Sustainable Development (Grupo de Formación e Intervención para el Desarrollo Sostenible [GRUFIDES]), 86, 99
Transitional Regional Board (CTAR), 99; environmental assessment by, 100
Tupac Amaru Revolutionary Movement (MRTA), 28
Two Perus, 34

UNAC, 99
unemployment, 5, 28
Unidad Nacional, 115
United Left (IU), 28, 29
United Nations Commissioner for Human Rights, 116
United Nations Office for Project Services (Oficina de las Naciones Unidas de Servicios para Proyectos [UNOPS]), 123
universities, described, 136
US-Peru FTA, 103, 106, 115
utility services, privatization of, xi, xii

Valdivia, Juan: on mining agenda, 137n3
Vargas, Gomer, 94
Vargas Llosa, Mario: art of rocking and, 35, 109–10
Vasquez, Isaías, 143n8
Velasco Alvarado, Juan Francisco, 46, 144n8
Velásquez Quesquén, Javier: DL 1090 and, 112
Vildoso Chirinos, Carmen, 112, 114

Villanueva, Edgar, 96
violence, 39, 145n15; level of, 133, 136; political, xxii, 28, 29–30, 38, 39, 43, 46, 128, 130

Wampis, 112
water supply, xiv, 24, 91; contaminated, 88, 127; disputes over, 23; environmental concerns about, 50, 100
water users' boards (*junta de usuarios de riego*), 22, 81, 94, 117, 142n3
weak institutions: democracy and, xvi-xvii; political competition and, xvi-xvii, xviii, xxi, xxii
Women's Affairs and Social Development Ministry, 114
work stoppage, described, 134
World Bank, 100, 143n10; complaints with, 86; IFI of, 99; Peruvian economy and, 33, 69

Yanacocha mine, 24, 95, 110; arrival of, 85–88, 126; bargaining roundtable and, 98, 100; dispute with, 86, 88, 90–91, 92, 94, 97; EIA and, 93; environmental concerns about, 88; experience of, 121; gold from, 84, 92, 103; as mega extractive project, 99; mercury spill and, 89–90; ownership of, 86–87; protests against, xxiv, 23, 100–101; response from, 88–89; TC and, 93; water pollution near, 100
Zamora, Andrés, 143n8
zinc, 48, 49

www.ingramcontent.com/pod-product-compliance
Lightning Source LLC
Chambersburg PA
CBHW021905020426
42334CB00013B/488